Finding Beauty

in the Crevices of Pain

Finding Beauty

in the Crevices of Pain

A Passage through Grief and Widowhood

MEMOIR

FELICIA G Y LAM

Published by:

Felicia G Y Lam

Email: felicialam7@gmail.com

2nd Edition

ISBN 978-0-9894751-4-3

Printed in the United States.

This book is dedicated to
the memory of my loving Husband,
love of my life, father of my children
and my Best Friend Forever

Gan Aik Ben

11 June 1957 — 5 January 2008

"Thank you for the best years of my life with you, Ben."

Table of Contents

Foreword

For many years, I have been teaching about grief, writing on the topic of grief, coaching people in grief, and whenever possible, reading books about grief. Reading *Finding Beauty in the Crevices of Pain*, however, brought about a response that was different than any book had before. As I read Felicia's story, I smiled, I cried, I reflected, I gave praise to God for the amazing way she shares her story of grief. It demonstrates the reality of grief. It gives hope in the midst of dark times.

The most beautiful part of this book is that it is Felicia's story. She talks about her real-life experiences, as she journeys through her grief. She is open and vulnerable, giving us a glimpse into her life through the years following the death of her husband. There is incredible beauty in all that she shares.

What I love is how much her story reflects what I teach in my classes at Coaching at End of Life. My books, *Coaching at End of Life* and *Coach Yourself Through Grief* are instructional. They instruct people in how to minister to those who are grieving. This book is Felicia's personal story, which perfectly illustrates all that I impart through my training. She brings to life what I teach.

This book has touched my life, and encourages me once again to make the most of each and every day.

Thank you, Felicia, for writing this book and for sharing your story. I have no doubt that many lives will be touched as a result of it.

Dr. Don Eisenhauer
Coaching at End of Life

Preface

Exactly ten years ago today, 5 January 2008, my beloved spouse, Ben, was called Home to be with the LORD. Special days hurt more, and I prefer that such days pass quietly. Why should one day be more important or special than the other, since not a day has passed since then that I have not thought of him any lesser than today?

The loss of a loved one is always painful and difficult because when a loved one dies, there is a sense it's just not real. You float through the next few days as if you are watching yourself from the outside.

You have no words to describe all that is going on inside your head. Every single response or experience you relate afterwards when someone asks how you are may only make up a tiny fraction of everything else that is screaming from inside of you.

All of a sudden, *nothing* seems to matter. The days ahead seem like a long, intimidating road, and you truly believe you can't make it alone for the rest of your journey.

Everything in your head seems to come to a stop—like a complete standstill in the middle of a massive traffic jam. You can't think or even make an apparently simple decision without your loved one. So you decide based on how he or she would have liked it done, if they were still here with you.

Every day, you wish you could trade places with your departed loved one because it is far more painful to deal with grief than death, itself. Unless you have gone through the pit of darkness and sorrow known as grief, you will not know what I mean.

When someone close to you dies, you don't just lose that person on the physical level. You deal with the loss of what might have been. Your pain involves missing that person's presence. It's not just sleeping in a bed that's half-empty, craving for the familiar company or an embrace, but knowing your loved one will miss all of the milestones in your life.

The tasks of sorting and packing their personal belongings, or dealing with the related paperwork in the following days will appear insurmountable at times. It is, after all, a closing of the final chapter of your loved one's life. It is inevitably difficult, yet necessary.

You may even feel a sense of impending chaos threatening to crush you under the weight of it all. *Don't* be intimidated. Start with one task and brave it through one by one. Every simple task you undertake will bring you further away from the first one.

Ignore opinions of people around you as you go through your own process of grief. No one but you, alone, knows how it is to be you and to grieve for someone you love. Every grief is personal and each has its own rhythm of pain and healing.

Each life story shared with a spouse is unique. Thus, not even another widow or widower may feel the same intensity. *Forgive* them for they know not what they are saying.

Take your time. Listen to the birds. Stare deep into the green of nature and return the smiles of the blooms that greet you. Plunge into the rivers of peace from God above. When nothing else makes sense, think nothing more of it. Like a little child, learn to lean on the One who holds your breath and knows the number of your days.

In *Eat, Pray, Love*, author Elizabeth Gilbert said:

> Deep grief sometimes is almost like a specific location, a coordinate on a map of time. When you are standing in that forest of sorrow, you cannot

> imagine that you could ever find your way to a better place. But if someone can assure you that they themselves have stood in that same place, and now have moved on, sometimes this will bring hope.

Each day will bring you closer to the promise that everything will get better because you survived. Taking a leaf of wisdom from Roy T. Bennett, author of *The Light in the Heart*, "The past is a place of reference, not a place of residence; the past is a place of learning, not a place of living."

A decade has passed, yet it feels like only yesterday: Ben, our two boys and I were going places and living our lives together. There are days that are still somewhat harder than the rest. There is no end to the ways I will grieve, and for how long I will grieve. Though just one finite event, this has changed everything for me. It remains a continuous personal loss that unfolds in new ways throughout a lifetime.

If I have learned anything from the past ten years, it would be this: I can still trust God, even though I don't have to understand everything else. I am determined to live every day with hope, and even in joy, knowing that because we are in Christ, the goodbye between us—is only for now.

1

The Grief Ride

"This is how we go on: one day a time, one meal at a time, one pain at a time, one breath at a time."

—Stephen King, *Bag of Bones*

I did not plan how I would handle my own grief. Even though I had prepared myself to some degree for his death, I never realised I could still be so ill-prepared for the loss and grief that awaited me.

I had no idea what feelings had slipped in unnoticed that had left me numb throughout the months that went by. I was merely existing and did not have much of an inkling of whatever else that was going on. It was as though I had found a door into another zone altogether.

It was similar to falling into a trance after being stuck with a broken record playing in your head for the longest time, so that you no longer knew it was there. Sometimes, it felt quite like being in the eye of the storm. Even though there was a calm region, I had a sense of impending turbulence close by.

At some odd times, I found myself reaching for the phone to call him, only to remember that I was at a funeral. *His.* I seemed to have suffered some kind of a mental impairment, as though

I was living between the world that was real and one that was not. Sometimes, I could not separate one from the other. It was tantamount to a merging of two worlds that were in close parallel to each other.

Occasionally, a certain smell or an everyday ordinary item, such as his favourite mug or a coffee spoon, would hit me so unexpectedly, it would jolt me up from the usual rut I had been in. Then it dawned on me that he was gone. Not here, or coming back. *Ever.* And I would find myself breaking down in tears all over again.

My mind was frazzled and clouded for most of my waking hours. Everything seemed to move in frames, racing back and forth between the times when Ben was here to the road of emptiness that lay ahead of me. Maybe I *did* prefer to stay in a giant nebulous ball of nothingness, so I would not remember the details that had brought me so much pain. I stayed in bed a lot and often wished it was all only a nightmare.

Some days, I woke to a perfectly beautiful and promising morning, where the birds were happily chirping away outside of my window and the dew-kissed flowers were gloriously blooming. Yet it would snap me down into shreds because I could not share it with him. On a horribly miserable day, everything felt worse in his absence, as he always knew what to say or do to make it all seem better.

On most days in the initial weeks, I would find myself staring into the cabinet where his clothes were. I would hold onto them and cry like a child who had just been abandoned. It was similar to a scene where an oncoming train was crashing into me again and again but I would still *not* move.

My own isolation for months in a familiar dark corner of my room that I called '*My World*' had brought me much solace and a sense of rest. In it, I felt that time was suspended. In it, I finally found a tiny space in this big wide Universe that belonged to me. I seemed to have no interest in whatever I was doing. I wanted to simply shut down completely: to sleep and never have to get up again. I just kept wishing there was a termination button I could hit.

The first three months were mostly spent doing the same activity I managed best. I found myself lying in bed a lot, listening to the sound of my own heartbeat. It was as if I needed to hear my heartbeat to remind myself that I was still alive, even though I could not feel it.

The guilt, I think, was the worst. In the first few seconds after I was told that he had died—even though there was a sickening reality of death—I was relieved because he was not suffering anymore. But soon afterwards, I began to feel a heavy sense of guilt for having felt that way. I was afraid if anyone knew how I really felt, I would be severely condemned for it. *How could I be relieved that he was dead?*

In the days and even weeks after the funeral, I barely spoke any more than was necessary, as conversations with others simply felt burdensome. Both for themselves and me. I looked forward to the luxury of retreating into my own solace whenever I could, often yearning for company and, yet, preferring none.

I had very little desire to speak to anyone about what I was really feeling because I was convinced no one would understand. And even if I wanted to, how would I speak about it when I could not even articulate what I was feeling? *Grief.* Like an enigma wrapped up in a riddle. Where do I *even* begin?

I could not even manage to complete a full sentence when I tried to write after a grief counsellor visited me and advised me to try journaling. I so desperately wanted to open up a window to let it all out, even if it was just a little at a time. But I could not even find a word to begin when I tried. I could not even pray.

It seemed bearable when I was not taking it in fully. Most times, I had to confront it simply because it made me angry enough to do something. It was hard to imagine being an object of love and God's goodness when you lose the purpose that had held the beliefs of your existence. You could cry all you want. But you just won't see it.

In Storm of the Century, Stephen King wrote, "When his life was ruined, his family killed, his farm destroyed, Job knelt down on the ground and yelled up to the heavens, 'Why God? Why me?' And the thundering voice of God answered, 'There's just something about you that pisses me off.'"

You could feel a sense of self-loathing, of blame, and even as though you were being punished. Sometimes, I felt so alone. It was as if I had fallen so far into the abyss of blackness and obscurity that I had reached the other edge of eternity with nothing else to hold on to.

I had simply lost the interest to live.

2

The Emotion of Missing Someone

"If you live to be a hundred, I want to live to be a hundred minus one day, so I never have to live without you."

—Winnie the Pooh

Day after day, I awoke to a world that felt empty to me. I could hear the birds singing outside my window when I opened my eyes; I saw the sun returning home in the evenings. I told the LORD, "I am ready to leave. I have no incentive to live on." But God seemed so cold and distant because I would still wake to yet another day and then another, as if I was being intentionally ignored.

It felt immensely void, parched for miles and miles away on a wide, free expanse of space. It was as if heaven and earth had met each other out on the horizon and you simply could not tear them apart. It was similar to walking on shifting sand, so one never quite knew how to retrace where you had been when the day was over. I just merely existed. It was a sad, meaningless existence—and I was in it.

Getting through the day and making it through the night was my greatest goal for each day. It felt so much like having a great story being rudely interrupted unexpectedly. It was as though someone had put a full stop in the middle of my book that had many chapters yet to go.

The emotion of missing someone is difficult because it has no promise of an end date or relief of any kind. The long nights alone were especially agonising. You just somehow make it through—like fighting a withdrawal of sorts, cold turkey, night after night.

I miss the sound of his car pulling into the driveway, the clanging of his keys hitting the door, and the familiar tune he would whistle when he came home every evening. I miss how our two sons and I would always fight for his attention during dinners, recounting to him the day's happenings. I miss the fun, the banter, the silly things we all did and said that only the four of us could understand why it was funny.

I miss his voice and the sound of his laughter. I miss the phone calls he would make in the day to remind me that he was thinking of me. He would call me so often in a day that it used to drive me crazy.

He was witty, funny and clever. I miss having the same special person with whom I could talk to about anything, no matter how insignificant, at the end of every day. He was also someone who was unpretentious, extremely kind and generous in both thought and deed.

I miss how he would always give me his undivided attention no matter how tired or busy he was. I miss the way he was always so fully present to listen, to resolve and how he always had an answer to everything.

Most of all, I miss being the first person he would always look expectantly to see when he arrived home from work every evening. A value I never knew existed until it was gone.

There were nights when I missed him so much—*so much*—that I would find myself drawn to the room he had previously occupied when he was sick. I often kept the door to this room slightly ajar, perhaps *still* somehow hoping to catch a glimpse of him again from the small opening as I passed by this room each day, content even if it was possible only through a figment of my imagination.

The Seduction of Suicide

There were nights when I couldn't sleep because I missed him so much that I would enter into the room quietly. I would sit in a corner in the shadows with my head on my knees hoping to feel whatever was left of his presence or to catch a whiff of the scent he had left behind. The yearnings were intense—so intense—that the prospect of escape via suicide often danced in seduction before me.

The execution of the act itself was not difficult, and it seemed to promise quick relief from all the pain and suffering that I was in. Have I thought of my children? *Yes.* I had even gone about quietly, setting things in order as if I was preparing to make the transition for them as painless as I possibly could. Yet I knew I would be forever ashamed had I left this way. Then an even more terrifying thought came to me. *What if—I'd killed myself, only to wake up in a different world from Ben?*

Perhaps I really could not dismiss the existence of God, despite it all. I still believe there is a God! And He could not have led me so far out here, only to abandon me now. I still hear myself saying in a stubborn whisper, *"Though You slayeth me, yet will I still trust in You."* [1]

Nonetheless, the sleepless nights were long and extremely difficult to get through. I simply could not describe the emotions that were consuming me by the seconds. Night after night, I battled through the tease to end the pain and agony in my soul. Yet it wasn't just any idea to be reckoned with, as executing it could cost me my soul.

I remembered my older sister, Alice, who was barely forty years old when she took her own life. I was only 18 at that

---

[1] Job 13:15 (New International Version)

time. Now at 39, I found myself passing through this familiar, precarious path that my sister had once taken.

She had come into this world expecting much, but all the bad breaks and heartaches of life had left her bitterly disappointed and empty. I remember how my sister's eyes would light up each time she talked about food, and how she would like to run a food business someday.

I could not help but spend years wondering where my sister had gone in the afterlife. Also, the person she could have become had she not quit on life that fateful day. I'd never once doubted that my sister was capable of achieving great success because she was extremely gifted, passionate, determined and such an incredibly beautiful person, inside and out.

It was without a shadow of a doubt that she could have fulfilled all that she was destined to be and more, had she only chosen to listen to the voice of hope rather than despair. Somehow, that made me *very* angry for her. And it made me even more determined *not* to let that same voice win again.

Journal

The emotion of missing someone is tormenting. It felt so much like drowning that I sometimes found myself gasping for air. On some mornings, I would wake up with chest pains as if to remind myself that my heart was hurting because it had been broken. I lay in bed with a blank mind, as emotionless as a corpse. Maybe I did wish I was dead and was *pretending* to be dead. But dead people can't feel pain—yet I *still* did.

One day, I sat up and began to write a little. I found that keeping a journal helped open up something inside of me that I couldn't speak about. Soon, my adolescent sons encouraged me to try blogging. I was quite glad that I did, as the response from the blogosphere was surprisingly encouraging. Many even wrote to me, sharing their own loss and pain. Many thanked me for writing because somewhere in my pain, they said it hit a note with theirs, too. Perhaps the validation of being heard and the need for connectedness *do* matter with the healing process.

At the same time, it baffled me that I could so easily tell my life story to complete strangers through my writings, yet it wasn't half as easy to talk about it to people who knew me in real life. Could it be that no one really likes to listen and everyone prefers to talk? The noise and chatter of supposedly well-intended advice only adds more clutter to an already restless mind. It struck me that I wasn't really looking for answers when I needed to speak about my pain. I just wanted to be *heard.* I thought of Jesus during his earthly ministry. He was a busy man, yet he always had time to listen.

It dawned on me that the world is moving at such a dizzying pace that most people are overwhelmed and overinformed. It is only natural that everyone needs to have his or her own filter and time they could afford to set aside for others. Thus, journaling is a personal indulgence without it being at the expense of someone else's time. After all, each of us only has a finite amount of time. It is only right to guard each second that ticks by thoughtfully and to use it in exchange for something eternal.

When I sit to write, I get to take my time to draw out from the innermost parts that really matter. It is only when the deepest things that are hardest to say are laid out in the light that the darkness loses ground.

As I began to find my voice in the process of expressing my heart's cries, I found the rope to reach for clarity in my thoughts once again. The prayers that I could not make in words, all the same, were often made through the tears that flowed as I wrote.

Then I had an epiphany: maybe everything that was painful and every broken piece in our lives that didn't make sense before was necessary because only God can bring the best out of our worst. Perhaps the grief, the sorrow, the despair, the loneliness, the isolation and even the silence in my world were *all* necessary; for without them, I would not have discovered that I could write with my heart. I wouldn't have a reason for it, otherwise.

The Holidays

The holiday season was not a particularly favourite time of mine. The poignant dark shadow of sadness seemed more acute during the holidays than at any other time of the year. Everything associated with the cheer of festivities just seemed to create a greater hole in the loss. I squandered most of such days by sleeping them away.

One weekend, I decided to accept an invitation to a local community grief talk. Everyone in the room had lost someone they had loved. The degree of pain in each may have varied but the sombre atmosphere in suffering a loss remained no less real.

As I gazed into each of those faces, I recognised the familiar deep pain that was etched in each of them only others like us could understand. Morrie Schwartz once said, "Maybe death is the great equalizer, the one big thing that can finally make strangers shed a tear for one another."

If I had not felt pain to such a degree, I would not have understood more than what I needed to know. I would have shrugged or turned off when the same topic was being raised again by the same person. I would have thought that such persons were merely attention seekers, and I should not encourage it.

I spoke with one or two couples briefly during the coffee break. None of us were really in any mood for a social chat. The silent understanding, smiles, nods and courtesies sufficed in putting us all in a very comfortable place of our own. It was as though each of us was living in an independent bubble of our own. We stayed afloat, day after day, until we would someday be ready to land our feet back on the ground once again.

His Belongings

Would letting go of his things begin the process of healing? I learned that those things were called 'linking objects'. As long as one keeps them, he or she will always be linked to the memories of the departed.

Every item that had belonged to him would quickly transport me back to the time when we had picked the item together, the funny things he had said, or the look on his face while we were in a shop or on a street somewhere. Memory after memory flooded my mind.

Even after many years had passed, I still could not bring myself to clear out his clothes to make room for my about ready-to-burst wardrobe. Time after time, whenever I opened his wardrobe to find some space to borrow for my clothes, I would be left crippled by the feeling of loss that I could not even move one thing away.

Even his toothbrush is still there in the shower where it had always been. Each time as I look at it in the morning while using the bath, I could not help but be reminded of what my grief counsellor had asked me before. "Do you think he will need it?" I couldn't answer that, *then*. Nevertheless, I know now—it is not for him, but for me that I am still keeping it.

The Castle of Our Love: Our House

The house he had built for us stands so quintessentially romantic as it is silhouetted against the sky during sunset or after a shower. The design is typical of a memorial shrine of an old-world palette that had been pulled out of a Rembrandt painting, reflecting Ben's love for the Tudor architectural style, which he probably developed during his student years in England.

Whether it was the oversized chandelier that was hanging in the family hall depicting the romance of the Renaissance glory, or a piece of customised furniture we had commissioned, each reflected our personal appreciation of a certain art period. Together, it resembled a dance of a perfect synchrony of two persons in love.

Most of the purchases, from customised furniture to personalised crafts, were made during his work in Jakarta for our dream house project. Although the quality and craftsmanship varied according to the price, it would be fair to say that we had gotten away with most of the treasures for a song. He was hard at work while I shopped even harder.

I hid away in my room most of the time after his passing. Perhaps I really was quite afraid to look at everything outside, as everything reminded me of him. Outside of my room, I saw Ben—whether it was in a meticulous line or in the curve of an object. I remember flashes of him going places with me. I remember how I would forbid him to utter a word whenever I was trying to negotiate a good price. He would often spoil it for me because he just didn't understand the art of haggling.

I thought of the story of the lovesick emperor who had built the Taj Mahal, a grand mausoleum of love displayed for his beloved queen. Each stone that the calloused hands of the builder had carefully planted into the masonry of the building had carried a sweet kiss of love, blessing and song. A love which would leave a trail even long after the hair of one's crown had turned silver, and the skin of the once fair and soft taut maiden had wrinkled and shriveled past the ravages of time.

Memories of the four of us echoed, danced and played in vivid images in my mind. Sometimes the shadows seemed to tease me as I walked down the hallway, past the spaces that now appeared so vast that emptiness enveloped the whole of me.

I hurried past them each day pretending that I did not see or hear them. The house where laughter had once emanated now lay silent and cold. Even the shadows that had fallen from the objects within the dwelling possessed a character and beauty of their own that was simply flawless in every way.

We were supposed to enjoy the house together, yet the loss of Ben stood out like a stubborn, poignant pain that would not go away. It was a loss accompanied by guilt that was simply too huge to ignore. The pain of Ben's absence seemed more bearable when we went about our day going through the motions, rather than truly living life in it.

Guilt

One evening over dinner with the boys, I blurted out of the blue, "I should have been a better choice …" but stopped short when I realised it would make the boys uncomfortable had I continued. It was a random line that had seemed to come out of nowhere, except a spillover from my own thoughts.

"Better choice for what?" one of my sons asked.

After some hesitation, I decided to make it known anyway.

"To have died."

That familiar awkwardness and silence filled the space that we were in. I had often tried to coax both my sons to speak about their own emotions of the loss without much success. Perhaps boys were just wired to be more logical in their thought processes rather than being incessantly emotional like their grieving mother. There had been too many good dinners that had gone bad between us. We could have done worse, had I not restrained myself to stay off the grief topic for most of our conversations around the table.

But then, this time the younger boy responded. He said to me, "No. If it'd been you who died … Papa would not have survived it."

What he had asserted offered me an enormous sense of comfort and inner peace. In that one-liner of a young boy, he echoed maturity and deep understanding of things. His simple answer had not only acknowledged my suffering, but also affirmed my strength—both, at the same time. Even though it did not immediately kill my morbid fascination with death ever since their father's passing, I saw guilt leave our house that day.

3

Meeting My Significant Other

"We're all a little weird. And life is a little weird. And when we find someone whose weirdness is compatible with ours, we join up with them and fall into mutually satisfying weirdness—and call it love—true love."

—Robert Fulghum, *True Love*

Scene after scene played out in my mind. I remember the very first time Ben and I met through a mutual friend. Ben had just completed his doctorate studies in England at that time. I was 18 and he was 29.

Even though he was eleven years older than me, our age difference had never bothered either of us. He was unlike anyone I had ever dated in the past. I felt grown up and safe with him. There was an innate, quiet charm about him that was extremely attractive.

About six months later, I left my birthplace in Melaka to work with our national carrier in Kuala Lumpur as a flight stewardess. Shortly after, he, too, left our quiet little town for a job offer in Singapore.

To be living away from home, paying my own rent and learning to be self-reliant as a young adult was rather intimidating, yet liberating at the same time. The culture of the job opened up a world of many different kinds of temptations as well as challenges.

Each time I had an awful day at work, it was him that I would call. He was attentive and always had a way of making me feel better.

Ben was a young engineer working for an oil and gas consulting firm. He would drive to Kuala Lumpur every weekend to see me. As time passed, I saw more and more qualities in him that I admired. We began to grow more attached to each other over time.

I would often swap my flight duties whenever they fell on a weekend, so I could spend that time with him. Sometimes, I would fly in to meet him if I had more days off during the week. He, on the other hand, would always choose to drive as he seemed to have an irrational fear of flying.

Being in a long-distance relationship made me realise how much I missed him when we were not together. Since it was to be only days apart before we would meet up again, I suggested we could write short notes instead of letters whenever we missed each other. He didn't appear keen on the idea and only said he wasn't the writer-type. I paid no attention to what he said and bought two pocket-sized notepads, anyway. Each mini pad contained about twenty-odd pages, and we kept one each.

Sometime later, he returned the notepad to me, every page filled with his scribbling. He told me that he had handwritten a page every night since I gave it to him, including the one night when the power had been cut and he had written by candlelight.

"So, where is mine?" he demanded playfully.

"Well … I guess I'm not the writer-type." I smiled sheepishly.

One weekend, our time spent with each other had to be shortened as I was scheduled for an early morning flight out that Sunday. Time seemed to slip away too quickly whenever we were together.

When I returned to my rented room after being away for several days, there was a sense of emptiness about it as I had missed him terribly. But then, I noticed a letter that he had left for me on my nightstand. I was left absolutely dumbfounded by the soul of his letter. He wrote:

Date: 15-5-88
Sunday
(6:15 a.m.)

My Darling Fel,

Couldn't sleep at all after you left. So went to make myself a cup of coffee (not as good as yours, of course). Come to think of it, even if you made rotten coffee, it would still taste as good to me. I have never imagined a supposedly rational person like me could get so emotionally attached to another person. In any case, I should thank my lucky stars (or our friend D) that I found you. Or, perhaps I have been a good person in my previous life(s). Even worse, maybe you were indebted to me in your previous life and now you are paying back in full. (Ha! Ha!)

Darling, please eat regularly and don't skip any meals because I want to live through to the ripe old age with you. Don't really know what to do if I have to go through life without you. I would very much like to bring our 30 grandchildren, 90 great-grandchildren, and 270 great-great-grandchildren, together with the prettiest and cutest great-great-grandmother, to K.F.C. during every school holiday. I think 30 grandchildren is about the most we can handle, right?

Looking forward to seeing you next Saturday. Please eat regularly. If you can't eat, at least please eat for me, o.k.? I can never find anyone to replace you. In any case, I don't want to find anyone to fall in love with. We are the original odd couple and I like it this way. I don't mind my friends now start calling me irrational.

Before I met you, they always said I was too rational to fall in love with any girl. Come to think of it, I was fortunate not to have met you then, or I wouldn't be able to complete my research. On the other hand, even if I met you when I was doing my research, you were still too young for me to be interested in, right?

I kinda like the term my friend used on you: Ben's Jewel. Of course you are Ben's Jewel. Who else could be appropriate and suitable enough to be my Jewel? You are worth all the travelling to K.L. every weekend.

I really long for the day when both of us could be together permanently. Tell your mother not to worry, I promise to marry her daughter when she agrees to marry me. (Ha! Ha!)

LOVING YOU,

ETERNALLY,

INDEFINITELY,

PERPETUALLY,

FOREVER,

IRRATIONALLY,

THOROUGHLY,

INTENSELY,

NATURALLY,

UNRESERVEDLY,

TRUTHFULLY,

WHOLE-HEARTEDLY,

EVERY PICOSECOND ($1/10^{12}$ second)

NANOSECOND ($1/10^9$ second)

MICROSECOND ($1/10^6$ second)

MILLISECOND ($1/10^3$ second)

SECOND

KILOSECOND (16.7 minutes)

MEGASECOND (11.6 days)

GIGASECOND (31.79 years)

TERASECOND (31709 years)

FOR THE REST OF MY PRESENT LIFE AND AN INFINITE NUMBER OF LIVES TO COME.

ALL MY LOVE AND KISSES,

BEN (7:15 a.m.)

XXXXX.....∞

4

Your Heart Will Know

"Love is not finding someone you can live with. It's finding someone you can't live without."

—Rafael Ortiz

If Ben and I had never been in a long-distance relationship, I would never have known how much I missed him when we were apart. I would never have been more certain that he was the one I wanted to spend the rest of my life with. Or rather, the one I could not live without.

As we continued to meet halfway week after week, each parting made me more determined than ever to close the gap. I couldn't stand the feeling that I could miss someone so much that it would consume me day and night.

I spoke to a number of colleagues about my intention to quit the airlines. Every one whom I'd spoken to advised me not to act impulsively. They reminded me the process from selection to training, and finally, to make it to flying had been undoubtedly challenging. They reasoned that it was every young girl's dream job to fly the skies, go places, meet people, and be paid well for it. They simply could not understand how I could give all that up in a heartbeat.

Everything they said to me made perfect sense. Yet my heart was telling me only *one* thing. And that is, I could not stand being apart from Ben for even another day. Despite my friends' persuasion advising me to stay on, my mind was set.

I called my mother one evening to tell her that I had quit the airlines. She didn't seem perturbed by it. When I went back home to see her some time later, I remember her telling me, "I am sleeping better during thunderstorms now."

I asked her why. I was not aware she had problems with insomnia or fear of thunderstorms before. I was surprised when she said, "About the same time that you'd started working for the airlines, I would feel anxious whenever there was a heavy thunderstorm. I always feared something might happen to the plane due to bad weather and that you might be in it."

I was taken aback as that was the nicest thing my mother had ever said to me! I had no idea she had been worried about me flying all that time, or at all!

The relationship between my mother and I had always been difficult when I was growing up. The same year after my father passed away, we went from emotionally distant to hostile after I told her that I had become a Christian. I was 12 when my father died of pancreatic cancer.

It was my neighbour who had shared the gospel with me. I went home excitedly one day and announced to my mother that I had decided not to burn joss sticks at the family altar any longer. I said, "Jesus-God does not want me to pray to other gods anymore."

Next thing I knew, she pulled me to the front of our family altar, yelling at me to kneel but I refused. Then I heard the familiar sound of the cane being whipped wildly in the air. It was the very first time I had made no attempt to run or shield myself from the blows. Nor did I even let out a sound.

Even though I was aware I could be inflicted with a lot of pain, there was a strange peace all over me that made me unafraid. I felt only love in my heart. She threw me out of the house but had a change of heart later. She went looking for me at my neighbour's house and took me back in.

It was years later that I watched the movie *Jesus of Nazareth*. It was the scene where Jesus was flogged and suffered great pain for my sins that reminded me of the day when I had stood up for Jesus in my family home. It struck me that it was the same love I had felt in my heart for Jesus! Because it was for love that Jesus came!

I remember trying very hard to win my mother's approval and affection over the years, only to regularly have my attempts be dismissed as insignificant or to have them undercut in some other ways. But things between us began to improve dramatically when I left home and moved to the city. Our relationship went through a slow but gradual healing process that grew stronger over the years until she, too, became a Christian.

She asked if I had any new plans after leaving the airlines. I told her that I wanted to move in with Ben and go back to school. I had always wanted to study law. In fact, that was what I had written down when our form mistress made us write about our aspirations in the career guidance form on the last week of school.

My mother didn't seem to mind whatever I wanted to pursue as long as I could self-fund it. But she was plainly against my idea of moving in with Ben, as she didn't want to risk me ending up with an unwanted pregnancy. It was either that Ben and I got married, or we should remain content dating and staying in our own separate places.

I knew that my mother made good sense. I was certain about my feelings for Ben but not exactly ready for something as final as marriage, itself. Nevertheless, hearing my mother say all those things that night gave me the feeling our relationship was mending, and I didn't want to spoil it. I had always craved her approval and love ever since I was a young child. I had always desired for her to be proud of me, and maybe, even love me in a way I could perceive it.

I told Ben about the conversation I had with my mother. He just laughed and assured me that should I ever get pregnant, it would never be unwanted. His parents would be over the moon if that happened, he said.

I didn't find his answer any more helpful because I was aware of my mother's concerns. Since we were so certain about each other being 'the one', I asked him if we should get married just as my mother had suggested. And without even a moment of hesitation, he just grinned widely and answered, *"Yes!"*

As unromantic as it might have seemed, at 20 or even for a 31-year-old, you don't always think things through. Otherwise marriage proposals, or an impulsive acceptance arising from lovesick fools, would have been a rare novelty.

You just jump off the cliff, experience the exhilaration, and simply hope that you are going to land safely when you hit the ground.

5

Marriage

"The bonds of matrimony are like any other bonds—they mature slowly."

—Peter De Vries

Getting our parents' blessings was the easy part. Staying blissfully married was the hard part. The wonder and excitement of living as one began to lose its appeal very quickly in daily mundane plans and domestic duties. I felt stuck in a humdrum of boring, repetitive and monotonous routine day after day. It was made worse that I had chosen to be a homemaker because *he* preferred it.

Every evening, he would glide into his La-Z-Boy and binge-watch television. He was fanatical about his MotoGP racing, or he could be laughing until he looked sick in the face watching *Blackadder*, a period British sitcom. I felt bored, lonely and left out.

Even though he would spend most of his time at home after work, we found that we didn't have as much to talk about like before. Friday was his beer night-out with his buddies, and quite often, even on Saturday evenings too.

It had always been that way even before I met him. Even though he did not mind taking me along, I never did enjoy the

Our wedding, in early 1989

noise, smoke or crowd in the drinking places very much. Since it was my choice to stay home, he could not understand why I was unhappy.

As he was not a Christian, we did not go to church. The fact that I was didn't make any difference to him because I never made a stand for it from the beginning. Our marriage did not magically subtract the things we didn't like about each other, at least not overnight. He was the same stubborn and hot-headed person who would rather choose meeting his friends over a beer or two on a Friday night than being home with me. And I was that same needy and insecure girl with too many emotional hang-ups, always craving attention.

I soon learned that he was a person of structure and habit. Once he had settled into a particular routine, he would be unwilling to deviate. Any slightest change would quickly upset him. He was also not the kind of person who appreciated surprises. He wanted to know the end even before he began anything. The rigidity and predictability suffocated me.

On the other hand, I was very much an impulsive person. To me, changes were fun! It was exciting to do something new because there was an element of surprise in not really knowing what to expect. I liked the idea of spontaneity and going to new places. I wanted us to try out new activities, meet new people and learn new things about the world around us together. I was at that age where life was just beginning for me, yet I felt as though my life was almost over. I soon realised he was everything that I was not. I was easily bored while he found comfort in predictability, keeping to everything that was chillingly familiar.

He was a homebody who was perfectly content with the familiar routine of being in front of the television every night. He didn't enjoy eating out because he always seemed on edge about the hygiene of the establishment as well as those who prepared his food.

If a certain food stall or restaurant pleased his standard for hygiene, he could go back to it every day and eat the same food.

There was one restaurant we would go to for breakfast every weekend. He was so predictable that even the servers stopped asking him for his order. They just put the order in and brought his food to him.

Once he related a story to me about a lady who sold *nasi lemak* near his office. *Nasi lemak* is a Malay fragrant rice dish cooked in coconut milk and pandan leaf. He said after some time, he needn't even get out of his car. She would pack it and hand it over to him every morning when she spotted him. He had that dish for breakfast every day for three months. He only started looking for other alternatives when that lady moved her spot away.

He also seemed to have an unexplained fear of onions, garlic and its close relatives, such as scallions, leeks and chives. Even though he could have them in food, they had to be finely minced and not be seen in their raw form.

On one of our shopping trips, we made a stop at the grocery section. I chose some fresh-looking shallots that were neatly packed in a small, red mesh bag and added the item into our trolley. Immediately, he reacted to it as though it was some biohazard substance and made such a huge deal about it. It was as if I was attempting to endanger our lives. I had to get them out of sight before he would finally stop agitating over it.

His behaviour was baffling to me. It was only years later when searching the Internet that I realised he had a valid medical aversion called 'Alliumphobia'. Many people with this condition have reported extreme anxiety and stress when exposed to garlic or similar plants with a pungent smell. Though it might seem absurd to those who aren't affected by it, nonetheless, it is very real to those who suffer from it.

Food choices aside, he made the most uninteresting travel companion anyone could possibly have. He would always be on edge about flying, being at airports and other unfamiliar places. I once asked why he was so afraid of flying. It was strange to me since he loved fast cars and superbikes. I know that because I had seen photos of him in thrill-seeking, daredevil motorcycle stunts where he did wheelies with his peers. He told me not having the control would make him jittery.

I became more and more unfulfilled over time because he always seemed agitated and stressed. Almost everything I did seemed to upset him. I thought it was my free spirit he found annoying, and as a result, I became increasingly offended and defensive.

I did not have the maturity at the time to realise he was simply a unique individual, just like me. He possessed traits and characteristics that made him the authentic person that he was. He had likes and dislikes, as well as irrational fears. Instead of showing more understanding and compassion towards his distress, I often allowed my mood to sour, always wondering what was wrong with him.

It escalated to the point one day that my mum noticed and asked, "Why do you seem so afraid of your husband?"

I answered defensively, "No, I am not. Who said I am afraid of him?"

She looked straight at me and said, "You are just not as enthusiastic about anything as you used to be."

On another occasion, my mum asked me, "Are you really happy after being married? A lifetime is not a short period. If you are unhappy, there is always a way out."

It was unusual that my mother would speak on this subject. Perhaps being raised the traditional Asian way, it was awkward to discuss emotions. Besides, I could not think of anyone who had been more unhappy and unfulfilled as she was with my late father. Yet she stayed with him until the end. Could that have been the reason for her concern?

Childhood

My mother reminded me more than once since I was a child that I was a mistake. Every time she was upset about something, she would express her wish that she should have terminated the pregnancy, killed me or given me away. She often voiced her disappointment at how the supposedly respectable and most experienced elderly town doctor who had examined her could have missed out detecting me in her womb. She would also question aloud through the years at how such a blunder could still be made even when she had clearly informed the good old doctor about her missed periods?

She recounted how she had found me naked and purple from the cold after the delivery only hours later because the hospital had stopped providing clothes for newborns. The nurses had simply returned me to the baby crib without even as much as a borrowed swaddling cloth. I could have died in the cold but I didn't. Quite clearly, I didn't have to be a clairvoyant to sense her disappointment about my existence.

Only now, I understood that I could not have died because the LORD had a purpose for my life.

I always felt I should have said something back to my mother each time she had spoken about it but it was always like a blank spot in my head. Only now, I understood that I could not have died because the LORD had a purpose for my life.

Had I died, then my mother would not have become a Christian, nor would Ben, our two sons and many others who God had raised me to stand in the gap for. It didn't matter whether I was instrumental or simply sowing in a word, love or prayer over their lives. Each birth is extremely precious because it has been purposed and sent out by the Creator's own breath and thus, is *never* a mistake in God's eyes.[1] The Scripture tells us that our frame was not hidden from Him when we were being made in the secret place and our days had already been written out before we were even born.

I could walk into the hall from somewhere and my mother's hostility would just ooze out without the need for provocation. I grew up in the kind of atmosphere where my two sisters and I were often cursed at and caned throughout our childhood, and even well into our teenage years, for the most illogical reasons.

When you are a child or even a growing adolescent, you don't understand what lies behind the words and actions done to you. You just *believe* what you hear by perceiving the directed emotions and actions. She was simply expressing her frustrations of feeling stuck in an unhappy marriage that saw neither hope nor any way out. We just didn't understand that the real issue *wasn't* about us, anyway.

But even so, it damaged our spirits. We remained broken and carried it into our relationships with other people. We become destructive until we come into the presence of God because only He is able to heal and restore us back into wholeness.

I went through much of my adolescence and young adulthood having a severely low self-esteem with a tendency to self-destruct, because when you hear something like this, something happens to your spirit. Words are powerful. Words harness energy that can both harm or heal internally, which affects the valuation and accuracy of one's worth and abilities whether you know it or not.

There was so much rejection and an inferiority complex in me that whenever I heard something complimentary, I would cringe and become uncomfortable. But whenever I heard something that was negative, even if it was clearly untrue, it would affect me so badly that I would let it become destructive to me.

I was just a little over thirteen when a boy kissed me on my forehead and said to me, "I love you" for the very first time. I

1 Psalm 139:15-16 (NIV)

responded with an emotional, "Thank you" and began to sob. He was extremely apologetic and weirded out as well when he asked why I cried.

I said, "I don't know. No one had told me that before."

Matrimonial Life

I always craved being loved by my parents, yet not knowing what love really is. I remember feeling quite lonely as a child as my siblings were all very much older than me. At twenty years old, I decided to take the plunge into matrimonial waters and simply hoped for the best.

Every time Ben and I had a disagreement, I would clam up the same way I did when I was growing up at home. As a child, I learned quickly that silence kept me safe from inviting more beatings from my mother whenever I sensed the tension in the house. But nothing would annoy Ben quite as much as when I did that. Perhaps he misunderstood my silence to be a retaliatory wall of aloofness rather than anxiety.

On one occasion, Ben was so frustrated with me that he picked up a footstool and threw it across the room. However, just before he could launch the throw, it hit the glass chandelier that was above him. The stunning piece that was embellished with the sparkling, faceted prism in pink teardrops shattered across the hall. I stood there in absolute disbelief and shock.

I ran upstairs immediately and locked myself in the bathroom. I remember crying, feeling quite afraid and confused at the same time. Although that incident was the very first time he had displayed aggression that scared me, it felt like déjà vu of my childhood all over again.

A few hours later, I came out of the bathroom when I felt the tension had diffused a little. He came up to me and apologised profusely for his behaviour. We learned to meet halfway more often after that incident. I learned that he appreciated open communication and that I could let him in on how I truly felt about anything at all.

However, his Friday beer night was still non-negotiable. Once I even said to him, "I hope I will *never* have a labour contraction or to have died on a Friday!"

I was convinced that if he had to choose, his friends would surely win hands down over me. Nevertheless, he would always reply with disbelief on his face, "Don't be ridiculous!"

A little over a year after we were married, I was pregnant with our first child. The obstetrician gave us the estimated due date for labour and what would you know? It had to fall on a *Friday*.

That day finally arrived. By evening, I overheard him making plans to meet up with his friends at the local pub over the phone. I stared at him in disbelief. He assured me that if a contraction kicked in, he would only be fifteen minutes away from the house.

It was December 1991, a time before every person had mobile phones. So he did the next most responsible thing. He left me the pub's contact number. I could not help but see the whole cast of *Cheers*, complete with their theme song, gracing the moment and coming to life in my mind.

As I sat alone in his parents' house that night, I kept looking at the time wondering nervously what one might expect from a contraction, and if I would know when it happened. I went to bed shortly after some light reading.

Just past midnight, I heard Ben come in. After washing up, he climbed into bed to sleep. Since I had been awoken, I felt an urge to go to the bathroom. I seemed to have a recurring urgency to urinate every five minutes or so, or whenever I tried to lie back down again. I was feeling increasingly uncomfortable all over.

Then it struck me. It *must* be that I was going into labour! I roused him as he was just beginning to fall into a deep, comfortable slumber. I wish I could admit that I might have been just a wee bit delighted for that sweet little revenge—but, *no*.

He jumped out of bed in a flash, obviously still looking groggy from his rather recent drinking session with his buddies. And like a true scout, he drove me as promised, burning some rubber along the silent streets in the wee hours leading to the maternity clinic.

A few hours later, our first child, Edward, was born into this world. He was so tiny, pink, perfect and beautiful. I had totally forgotten that I was supposed to be mad at his father for the incident a few hours earlier when he had chosen his friends over me.

The arrival of our first child had undoubtedly brought much excitement, especially for Ben's parents, as he was the first grandson born to their side of the family. Even I could not help but feel my own maternal instincts beaming through. I felt grown up, at last.

6

Parenthood Matures Us

"When you know better, do better."

—Maya Angelou

I loved being a mother even though it was a feeling that was completely new to me. I felt a sense of unexplained significance, awe and gratefulness for something so powerful and miraculous within a human body that it had the capacity to create another life.

I spent most of my waking moments for the first month just staring in awe at this beautiful little baby who had once stayed in my womb. Watching his tiny fingers grabbing onto mine, his smiles, coos and gurgles reminded me how much I was needed. My maternal hormones would simply go into a crazy overdrive whenever I held him in my arms.

It was as if I was looking at a second chance to fix the childhood I never really had. I aspired to be the kind of mother that I always dreamt of having and, thankfully, I did in the end. God gave me my mother back, made new.[1]

After my mother gave her life to Christ, the transformation was like day and night. The mother I grew up with did not know

[1] 2 Corinthians 5:17 (NIV). Therefore, if anyone is in Christ, he is a new creation. The old has passed away, behold the new has come!

Christ yet, so she never encountered the kind of love that could satisfy her need to be loved and to complete her. She had a troubled and unhappy relationship with my father that affected the way she had brought us up. It's true what they say – *hurt people hurt other people.*

Being a new mother, I began to have a deeper appreciation for my mother as being the woman who had birthed me. I once asked her why she never left my father since she was so unfulfilled. She expressed something to me that I will never forget. *"Every time I had enough courage to leave, there was a small child who needed me."*

We could have been continually caught in that vicious cycle of losing more generations to being destructive had it not been for the mercies of God intervening, turning us into a new generation who healed instead of hurt. I saw no benefit for blame as she simply could not give what she never had or knew. Sometimes, love just finds its way home a little later—at least, for some of us.

Parenthood

There were places we would never have gone and conversations that would never have taken place if we never had children together. By the time our second son, Edwin, was born five years after his brother, our marriage had reached a plateau of stability as never before.

Ben would call me every day from work, even when he was five minutes away from home. When he had to go abroad for work assignments, he would call me minutes after he had entered a cab. He would call just before boarding and upon arrival. He would call when he reached the hotel and just before he went to bed. He would call me so often in a day that it used to drive me crazy.

Our marriage became better and better over the years. It was Pope John XXIII who said, "Men are like wine—some turn to vinegar, but the best improve with age." Ben had certainly matured incredibly well. He was, to me, the very best kind. He treated me as though I were a queen, and naturally, I lived up to my role by returning to him the same royal service!

I was assured of my significance to him through his daily choices and actions. Ben wasn't the kind who was comfortable expressing the three little words *'I love you'* thoughtlessly, or without often cringing a little whenever he had to say it. Perhaps he'd found them such a worn-out phrase that the use of euphemism could replace a certain dulling certainty of platitude. Thus, he often returned in a rich, low macho voice, *"Yup, me too!"* To compel him further would only produce more unintelligible mumblings of a grown man. I have learned to appreciate that love in action was far better than the utterance of empty, meaningless words.

As his car pulled up to the driveway after work every evening, the foliage outside our home softened the white stucco walls of the house, providing a welcoming feeling to him. Even though it was not a large or fancy estate, it was our very first home together. A 'working house', as one would describe it. It was the starter home in which both of our children grew up and where some of our best memories were made.

From the inside of our home, we could already hear his familiar whistle at the door. The first thing he would always ask our children when they ran out to greet him was "Where is mummy?" He would put his briefcase down, hug the children or tousle their hair playfully. He would make his way into the kitchen or wherever I was and plant a kiss on my lips with puffer pout precision.

He would then proceed to his favourite cosy corner in the garden with his mug of hot coffee. There, he would go through his mail or relax with Edwin on the garden swing until it was time for dinner. Edward, the older boy, was always the one serenading us in the background on the piano in the evenings. The familiarity set a tone of stability within the home that was both very pleasant and soothing for everyone.

Ben always looked so cheerful whenever he arrived home after work that it had never really occurred to me if there was a bad day at the office. Although I might not have understood

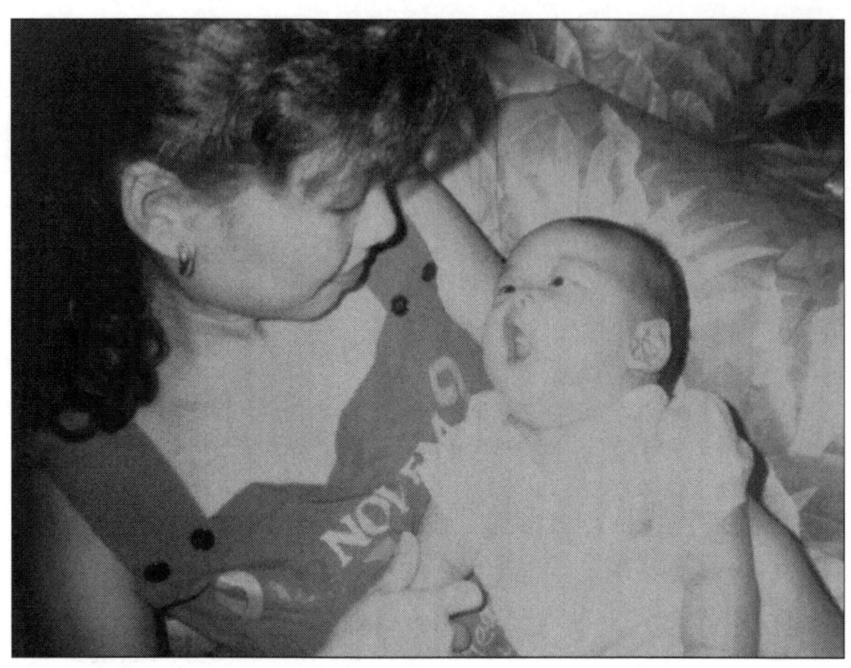

Our first-born, Edward, in early 1992

Ben (middle) with his sons, Edward (left) and Edwin (right) in 2002

his work challenges, I was often aware of the low points or periods that he had. Being a homemaker, all I knew best was simply to offer a restful and safe sanctuary for him to come home to every day.

I also enjoyed watching him eat. He would never fail to express appreciation in every morsel of food I had prepared. Even if he had faked it, I would still have believed it because he was that convincing.

I would always be grateful that our two young sons had lived and grown up in an environment where they were familiar with a father's display of affection for his wife and children. It provided them with a sense of emotional security that was necessary for a healthy development in their growing years.

He was such a loving man who I never had to demand or make known my wishes. He would often pull me close to him with his lips pouted and ask me on a weekend, "Tell me. What is your wish for today? Your wish is my command!"

And I would always reply excitedly, *"Shopping!"*

He would hold that look of eager enthusiasm while his frozen smile and eyes would often betray the slightly despondent emotion to the request. I could perceive how much he hated shopping. Yet he would always go along with it simply because he knew how much I enjoyed it.

He was loving, considerate, patient and immensely protective. He was more willing to make adjustments and try out new activities or places if plans changed for the day. He would take it in stride whenever something unexpected happened, when in the past, we would both get so uptight.

Ben could wait patiently for hours each time I went shopping. Not once had I heard him complain that I was taking too much time or been spending too much. Even my mother and my brother's wife, Susan, would often compliment me on his endearing, charming side, to which I would reply in jest, "Yeah ... I've trained him pretty well, haven't I?"

I began to enjoy his company more and more over time. I loved that he was always so fully present in every moment and not having his mind someplace else. If he was committed fully to work, it was no different when he showed up at home, too. We spent most of each night chatting with each other until one of us fell asleep. We talked about our dreams, aspirations for our children, things we could do together after his retirement, or just about anything. Sometimes, we revisited our childhood memories together, but mostly we talked about current things and future plans.

He said that before he met me, he did not have a reason to work hard or do anything more than he already did. He could have chosen an easy life by staying in the family business, as his parents would have very much preferred. Instead, he pursued work outside and remained true to his interests at heart and passion in the field of engineering until the end. Even though he did not always have good days at work, the sense of satisfaction and accomplishment that I could see in his eyes at the end of every workday told me that he had made the right choice.

"My parents must have been quite relieved at how I turned out in the end," he muttered with a quiet pensive smile.

"I know they are proud of you, Ben," I assured him.

In his silence, I understood that there was the child in him who had always looked up to his father, yearning for his approval, and to his mother for the nurture, support and understanding that no one could ever take their place. I guess we never really grow up, even though we mature whenever we are in the company of our parents.

Over time, I had also become more relaxed about his beer nights out with his buddies. Instead of resenting that he would prefer the company of other people, and not our children or me on a Friday or Saturday night, I began to show more understanding. As I grew more secure emotionally, I relieved him of the burden of having to choose between the two things that he found closely significant to him.

Once, he thanked me for rescuing him from being a bum. I was puzzled. He thanked me—for me and the gift of bearing his two children. He thanked me for turning any house we had lived in into a home for him and our children, no matter where we were. He thanked me for giving him a reason to work hard and to fulfil life at its best. Most of all, he thanked me for domesticating him. It was a feat he had never imagined was humanly possible, in his case at least, but I did it, he said. It felt strange to hear him say all that when *I was the one* he had rescued!

Perhaps a good marriage between two individuals is easy when you only need to focus on being *one*. In our case, he was the head and I did what I do best naturally, which was being the heart of our home. I valued that he had never compelled me to respect his position of authority, but he'd simply loved me into submission.

And everything else simply fell beautifully into place with ease.

7

Life Happens While You Are Busy

"Life is what happens while you are busy making other plans."

—Allen Saunders

Ben had always dreamed of building our own home together. When he told me that he was ready to purchase a nice plot of land that he had seen and liked very much, we were truly convinced it would be an exciting project we could embark on as a family. I pictured a stone-clad cottage home – one that invoked the warmth of the old-world charm of Tudor architecture, graced with exuberant foliage and vibrant, joyful blooms.

We had a huge dream but only a small budget. The construction began after months of work with our architect and finding a builder. Ben took care of the technical details while I worked on the aesthetics. We couldn't have found a more perfect partner in each other because he was someone who could see numbers in his head, while I only saw colours in mine!

The site supervisor assigned by the builder to our project was a quiet, responsible and excellent fellow. We enjoyed the site visits and the building process in the first quarter. But things at the site started to go off track when the supervisor left due to some personal issues. We took the initiative to spend more time at the

Building our dream house project together in 2005

Construction site, 2006

site so that the project would not suffer delay and design errors until a replacement could be arranged.

Unfortunately, we had not anticipated that so many problems and obstacles would arise during the construction stage. We realised only too late that we were totally unprepared for it. We were constantly anxious, stressed out and drained by all kinds of issues arising from financial costs to human relations.

Almost towards the end of the building project, Ben started coughing persistently for more than two months. We thought nothing much of it at first. He had consulted as many as four doctors, and all of them said it was probably caused by the dust exposure at the construction site.

None of them had thought of running a full medical screening on him, as his last full examination had the 'all clear' and had been done slightly less than a year ago. By the third month, it was getting unbearable. He could not work properly during the day nor get proper sleep or rest during the night. He was utterly miserable.

I suggested he should probably visit the last doctor for a further examination instead of consulting a new medical specialist every time he had completed the medication. He agreed and went back to the last pulmonary specialist to run some tests.

We received the news later that week. The biopsy report confirmed what we had feared most. We were told that it was lung cancer at stage 4. News of Ben's health issue came as a total shock. That day also happened to be his *birthday*. It just felt cruel.

The medical specialist explained to us that stage 4 was an advanced stage, which meant that cancer had spread to other areas of his body.

"How could this be?" I asked the oncologist. "Shouldn't we start at stage 1? Otherwise, why would you need stages 1 to 4, if you had just skipped right through to 4?"

As the doctor explained, Ben kept staring in my direction with a deeply concerned look on his face the entire time. I could tell that, even then, he was more worried at how much his illness would affect me rather than him.

More than once, I overheard our older son, who was 16, asking his younger brother, who was then 11, if he had finished his homework or showered as I passed by their rooms. Though the children and I had never discussed their father's illness, nor had we addressed the emotions that we were each going through during that time, there was a sense of pride knowing that my children were learning and developing valuable life skills and empathy in the midst of it.

We were advised to begin treatment as early as possible. I was not at all prepared for the new challenges and demands that came with the caregiving role. Nor did I anticipate that I would be required to accommodate far more than realistic expectations of people around me when I was in that capacity each day. I was stressed out, sleep-deprived and absolutely drained. Yet it wasn't an experience that one could talk about without it ever sounding immature or selfish.

Caring for my husband was a privilege because he would have done it for me, had it been me in his place. It was so physically and mentally challenging as everyone around us seemed to see only the one who was sick, but not the one giving the care, as if the caregiver spouse was visible only when required for the task.

I missed the support, intimacy and the husband I knew, who had once been so strong and healthy. Even though he was here in the flesh, he wasn't really here. I could only imagine how afraid and lonely my husband must have been in that state of illness. I understood it because I was feeling the same, though not completely from the same place. But what really upped the intensity most was that we had just moved into the new property. We hadn't even unpacked yet.

8

When You Become Your Spouse's Caregiver

After the initial shock had set in, we quickly focused on the oncologist's advice for the cancer treatment. One week after Ben had undergone his first chemotherapy treatment, he said he wanted to go shopping. That was new because I thought that line belonged to me.

I used to joke with my friends that when we went shopping, I'd shop till *he* dropped. But he would always refute it, "That's not true. You hardly spend. Besides, you make me happy when you do." Now how do you beat that one? On that note, I remember a marriage quote which read, "We always hold hands. If I let go, she shops."

So shopping we went. Ben decided to get himself a Beatles' look-alike hairpiece after we were told that he would experience hair loss when the cancer treatments begin. Next, we headed to a fitness store, and he ordered a treadmill that took almost a quarter of the floor space of a room. It cost around USD $1500, and even though I knew it wasn't that good an idea at that time, I remained supportive and let him proceed with the purchase.

I understood why he wanted it even though he never said it. We both knew he would be too weak for anything rigorous in the weeks or months ahead. We could wait to get it. But I also understood he wanted something that he could look forward to. He needed to be encouraged and motivated enough to fight this awful disease, and still have *hope* to be able to use it when he gets well.

We spent most of our time in the following weeks and months travelling back and forth to the hospital. There was always another medical test, chemotherapy session or radiation treatment. The hospital stays were equally as dreaded. In spite of it all, he remained optimistic and kept his humour.

I imagine he must have entertained the thought that he might die from the disease, even though he was innately a very optimistic person. I often sensed the unsettled emotions and fear in him. And why shouldn't there be?

Death puts an end to our life, our loves and our dreams. There is a deep, cold sense of finality that stings. Ben was quite contentedly an agnostic up to this point and had very little concept of the understanding and interest in the afterlife.

The cancer treatments left him persistently fatigued, but he still fought through several rounds of *septicaemia*[1]. It was often disheartening to find more medical procedures awaiting him as he woke to a failing organ, one after another. If it wasn't this, it was something else. We had only bad news and more bad news, all the time. However, the network of support from family members and friends in the initial weeks helped immensely, as it was easy to be tempted to look at the bad and expect the worst.

Watching Your Loved One in Pain

It was really difficult to stand by and watch all those needles, probes and tubes on him even for another minute longer. I remember asking the doctors if he would be well again if I gave him one of my lungs? If kidneys could be transplanted, why not lungs? The

1 Septicaemia is a serious bloodstream infection or blood poisoning that can quickly become life-threatening. It occurs when a bacterial infection elsewhere in the body such as in the lungs or skin, enters the bloodstream.

doctors simply shook their heads emphatically and told us that not all lung cancers could be treated the same way.

I remember praying and pleading often that God would let me be the one to stand in Ben's place. But God seemed distant. One might expect that God would have to attend to matters that were of a greater magnitude in the universe than hearing small petitions such as mine.

I remember the feeling of utter helplessness as I stood by his hospital bedside watching, as he went through every one of those horrid tests or medical procedures *every single day*, as though he was a lab mouse. They would turn his frail body this way or that, as if he was a rag doll. The discomfort and pain that Ben had to endure was incredibly tough. But the agony that I felt from *watching* him suffer, that was the worst.

At the Hospital

One of the unwelcoming side effects of the chemotherapy was managing the tiredness. Most of the time, he would be resting or sleeping. It cheered him whenever I would climb into the tight hospital bed with him to watch TV or read to him. Sometimes I lay next to him quietly, offering him the warmth and comfort that I was simply there with him.

Every now and then, the nurses would come into the room to monitor his vital signs and record them on the medical chart. The nurses often greeted us cheerfully and called us lovebirds. Ben, on the other hand, would return a cold unfriendly frown and squint at the nurses for taking his temperature and blood pressure. He was always quite kindly towards them but not if our snuggling time was being interrupted.

Ben and I often communicated using subtle signs such as hand and finger codes, eye signal exchanges or facial expressions whenever it was not convenient to say them aloud. It could be as ordinary as a slight squint or a "knowing look" thrown across a room. Even though most were common universal signs that people use, we did have several signals that were developed and personalised over the years.

I taught him the *Stone-Water-Bird* game, which was one of the variants of the more commonly known *Rock-Paper-Scissors.* It is a hand game in which each player simultaneously forms one of three shapes with an outstretched hand. We would play to decide who would do the task when we were either too tired or just feeling lazy and simply wanted to call for a pass. I was usually better at this by guessing correctly the sequence or odds of what he would use each time and would always beat him to it.

He got better only years later after he trained himself to be more unpredictable and erratic in the choices he would throw out every single time. It always made us laugh so hard irrespective of who won or lost in the end. Best part of all, he would, in the end, perform the task for me even if he had won. It was a silly childish game, but I miss this about us because no one else would be able to make me laugh quite the same way as only he knew how.

Our Nights Apart

During his stay in the hospital, our texts to each other kept us closely connected and encouraged. From Ben's text messages to me, I sensed his deep loneliness of being in this disease that was made worse by our physical separation. He often expressed his wish that he would much rather be at home, an environment where it was more comforting and familiar to him.

But gradually, he began to lose the ability to text anything back. Each time when I felt like I was losing my grip on things, I would scroll up to find his older texts reminding me how much I was needed to stay strong for him.

His texts asserted his need to battle the disease: *'You have been a great support to me. I wouldn't know what I would have done without you.'* Or the one he sent me just before being wheeled into the

Intensive Care Unit (ICU) telling me, *'Don't worry, I never plan to go without a fight for the sake of my darling wife.'*

He kept his word and made a quick recovery each time he had to stay in the ICU to fight another infection. However, the relief was often short-lived, as he would develop yet another infection due to the drop in his white blood cells from the round of strong antibiotics a week or two later. It was always like seeing him come out from one end of the tunnel only to enter into another one.

The Recuperating Room

When Ben was back home from the hospital, we would stay in the guest room on the ground floor, as he eventually became too weak to climb the stairs to our bedroom. Even though it was not the most comfortable room in the house, it was cosy enough. It even had a great and expansive view of green around us.

He spent less time sleeping than he would in the hospital. Sometimes, he would watch a movie with the children or even sit up to manage some paperwork. I liked it better when he was home, as I was able to cook and manage more chores without the guilt of leaving him alone at the dreary hospital.

One of the side effects of chemotherapy is the loss of appetite, which often posed a challenge in getting him to eat anything. I would suggest all kinds of food or liquid supplements that he might be able to handle, but none appealed to him. In fact, even the thought of food would make him nauseous and my frequent probing on the subject of his eating often irritated him greatly.

One afternoon, when I was trying to prepare lunch for him in the kitchen, my thoughts began to unravel as I stared out of the window. It was a hot and bright day outside with hardly any shadow or sight of an overcast sky even from afar. Yet it did not match the sad, dismal feeling of hopelessness that hung over me.

It didn't take long before I was standing by the sink crying like a little child. I did not even realise he had walked in until I felt him come up from behind and whisper in a soft hushed voice, "Hey … " he began, but was short for words himself. Then he wrapped his arms around me from the back. He held me close in his embrace while I cried my heart out.

As the lung cancer progressed, his voice became increasingly hoarse, altered and weak over time. We had to rely on a bell if he needed anything. It just seemed so wrong for someone such as him to lose his voice, or health, as there was still so much more in him to be said and done.

He really was an interesting person with such a brilliant sense of humour, wit and wisdom that was simply exceptional. And even though he had to struggle just to speak a few words each time, he still managed to say something funny by making light of the situation, or even slip in moments of tenderness where he would always remind me how beautiful I looked.

9

Collecting Moments

"Cancer changes your life, often for the better. You learn what's important, you learn to prioritise, and you learn not to waste your time. You tell people you love them."

—Joel Siegel

C*arpe diem* is a Latin aphorism, usually translated as *'Seize the day!'* It is a little like holding out your hand to catch the rain. You are aware of every drop that touches the palm of your hand even though you cannot retain it for very long. And that was how I felt about the minutes that ticked by too quickly when I was with my loved one suffering from his advanced illness.

One late afternoon, I remember placing my face very close to him while he was lying in bed. He had one hand wrapped around mine while he rested, as usual. His hand was large compared to mine. There was a comfort we both could not describe as we held onto each other's hand. As time on the life clock slowly ticked away, we became more and more aware of how little time we had left to express the bond of love between us that was still possible through physical touch.

I watched his frame slowly reduced into a weak and frail form from the effects of cancer, chemotherapy, radiation and drugs. It was a giveaway of a sad, hollow and distant look of a man who was once so strong and healthy. As I stared deeply into his medium brown eyes, I was intrigued by how beautiful his eyes really were. It was as though I had stared right into the depth of his soul.

I saw sadness reflected from deep within. I could not help but ask him, "How did you … even possibly … and could ever … have put up with me, for all these years?"

I thought of all the times that I had been petty and unlovable. I remembered all my failings in which I had made his life difficult. I felt so ashamed and only wished I had been more mature to have avoided all those selfish, childish tantrums that he had often patiently put up with.

Ben stared back into my eyes lovingly. Perhaps he could see my vulnerability. Instead of brushing it off with a weak 'it's okay' or something, he replied, with his brows slightly lifted and his eyes so haunting, "How did *you* … put up with *me*?"

I simply couldn't quite decide, afterwards, if Ben had just astounded me to some degree with such uncanny eloquence, or if it was the deep degree of pain that I felt because it had been so profoundly poignant and intense.

I had never met anyone quite like him. He was in every way a man, yet almost divine. The goodness that he exuded so often commanded attention, as people seemed naturally drawn and magnetised to him. He was innately charismatic and had the ability to look straight into one's eyes and evoke emotions that could touch one to the core with his sincerity or rebuke.

Where Do We Go After We Die?

I tried many times to tell him about the God of the Bible whom I had encountered when I was 12 years old. Unfortunately, this was the only part of my life that he absolutely had no interest in nor did he want any part of it.

Jonathan Foer once said, "Time was passing like a hand waving from a train I wanted to be on. I hope you never have to think about anything as much as I think about you." I imagined what it would be like if Ben were to leave this earth without knowing Christ, and for every day—for the rest of my life—I would live to regret it.

People often say, "I'm sorry for your loss" to someone they know whose loved one has died. But suppose we said, "I know where my loved ones are, and more than that, I *will* find them in a far better state someday," would we, hence, still call it a loss?

As I prepared myself to open the lines into the subject of the afterlife, I expected him to react with displeasure, and even risked him getting mad at me. I paced up and down the hallway of the hospital strategising how to speak to him about it. This seemed like such a bad time to upset him. But then again, would there ever be a better time for a topic such as this?

I proceeded to ask him what he thought about people who leave this earth and where would they go?

He answered thoughtfully that when a person dies, everything would just end. No heaven or hell, or anywhere in between. Just nothingness.

I asked him gently, "But, what ***if***—there is?"

He didn't say a word nor did he try to stop me from speaking further, as he usually would whenever we were on this subject.

I continued, "What *if*—you leave this earth only to wake up to find there really *is* a heaven and a hell? What *if*—the only people who believe and accept Jesus are the ones who really go to heaven?"

He replied that wouldn't be fair. There was no tolerance in that statement and that all religion teaches good—but *not* all Christians are good.

I looked at him apologetically and asserted, "It is true that not all Christians are good. Christians are human and they go to heaven not because they are good, but because they are forgiven."

I paused as we both sat in the room with intense silence for the next minute or so.

"What have you got to lose to believe …?" I probed. For the first time, he seemed to be listening with his guard down.

I continued.

"And isn't it better to wake up assuming there is a heaven than to find out that there is a hell? And suppose what you have guessed is right: that there is only nothingness in the end, and all that I've ever said is proven to be wrong—even then, you still have nothing to lose."

He fell silent, thinking deeply.

Although this was not the first time I had tried to raise this subject, it was the first time he had allowed me to speak this far on it. He kept his gaze down on the carpet floor as if he was staring into a bottomless void.

I looked at him sadly and continued, "You are aware our two sons and I are Christians, right? It means: we will never meet again if we died—as we will be separated to different places in the afterlife."

Then something I said seemed to have struck a nerve with him like never before. He shifted his gaze and looked up at me immediately. His eyes betrayed a sense of frantic loss as he realised the depth and breadth of the finality of our separation – *for eternity*. He gave a resolute look and affirmed aloud that he, too, wanted to be a Christian, so we could all be together again one day in the afterlife.

Even though his motivation for his decision, I suspect, might not have been from a place of faith at that point, it was a sensible and well-calculated gamble.

Parents' Blessing

Ben came from a very close-knit family. Naturally, he was concerned that his parents would be hurt by his conversion to Christianity.

He did not want them to misunderstand that his acceptance of a new faith would mean disloyalty and abandonment towards them. We expected a strong resistance from his parents, as they were staunch Taoists. We could only hope for their understanding, but were prepared, somewhat, if they didn't. So we were very surprised, of course, when his parents gave their permission right away.

I could see the look of relief on his face after the phone call with his mother. It was as though a great weight had been lifted off his shoulders. Yet no one could possibly be happier than me! In fact, I was *so* happy, I had to restrain myself from dancing to the whole rendition of *Macarena* all over the hospital hallway that afternoon!

Two pastors and several church leaders came to the hospital later that week and led Ben through the *Sinner's Prayer*[1]. He was baptised that afternoon by the sprinkling of water. Ben smiled and looked cheerful throughout even though he had to be confined to bed due to the illness. In the natural state, nothing seemed to have changed. He was still weak and stricken with a debilitating disease. Yet we sensed a certain lightness and tangible peace in the room afterwards. The fear and heaviness that had hung over us for the past months were quite evidently absent.

A sinner's prayer is significant in the eyes of God and to the spirit realm. The spirit realm recognises those belonging to Christ and those who don't. The Bible says that those who believe in Him are marked and sealed with the Holy Spirit, by whom is a deposit guaranteeing the inheritance until the redemption of those who belong to God.[2]

An East Malaysian friend once related to me the testimony of a former *bomoh* (local witch doctor) who had recently accepted Christ. The man was known to have the ability to look into the spirit realm. Many from the village would engage his services for

1 The Sinner's Prayer is a prayer a person prays to God when they understand they are a sinner and in need of salvation through Jesus Christ.

2 Ephesians 1:13-14 (NIV).

his dark arts, commonly known as 'black magic'. It was interesting that he noticed how evil spirits would tend to avoid those who were believers of the Christian faith. But then, those same spirits would easily attach on to those who were not. He recognised that those belonging to the Christian faith had a powerful spiritual covering, which the non-believers did not have. He was so taken aback that he decided to embrace Christianity himself and abandoned his dark practices after that.

Salvation remains central to every heart of a Christian who has loved ones who are still not saved, because life on earth is not all there is to it. Time on earth, or the created world, as Sir Thomas Browne puts it, *"is but a small parenthesis in eternity*." Nothing can be better than spending eternity with a loving God in a perfect new world and being reunited with our loved ones again in it! It is the hope of every believer in Christ that someday, all manner of sufferings of this life will end, and that He shall wipe every tear from their eyes. There will be no more death or mourning or crying or pain, for the old order of things has passed away.[3]

3 Revelation 21:4 (NIV).

10

The Last Days of Life

Since Ben's acceptance of his new faith in Christ, death was no longer something to be feared because heaven is better than here. It was for love, all the more, that I ought to let him go instead of compelling him to live on in suffering simply for our sakes.

I suspected he had passed up several chances of divine invitations that had come to him from heaven, itself. He once told me about being in a tunnel and how he had decided to turn back. On another occasion, he spoke about seeing many photographs of people he knew in his lifetime on the ceiling. Was he seeing parts of his life flashing before him as his soul was preparing to leave his body, but he had *willed* it to stay somehow?

When I was back home in the privacy of my own room after returning from the hospital, I could only cry out to God. Yet I was at a loss at what to pray or ask God for our situation. To ask for recovery at such an advanced stage defies my understanding. But I asked for a miracle, anyway. To ask God to take him would seem like a solution for him but then, what about us? I could not imagine the world without him in it, yet I could not bear the world that kept him in such a state.

I continued to see him hanging on stubbornly in spite of all the pain beating down on his body with not much hope or optimism. The days wore on as his organs began to shut down, one by one.

Then the wait began.

I went to his bedside one afternoon. I told him if he needed to hear me say the words, or if he needed my permission, I was ready to set him free. As Maya Angelou said, "Love liberates, it doesn't bind."

He was deeply sedated and remained in an unresponsive state in the high dependency room. I held his hand and told him not to worry about our boys as I would look after them. I gave him a promise I would love him forever, and he had my permission to let go. I am setting him free.

On the first day entering into the New Year of 2008, the doctors told me that his heart had stopped earlier, but they had successfully revived it. They told me that he would go into another cardiac arrest and needed to know if we were prepared to let him go, or have him connected to life support should his heart fail again.

As most of Ben's organs had shut down, the choice seemed clear his appointed time was close. The doctors and I agreed it would be more dignified to free him from more pain and suffering, as his condition clearly would not benefit any further with such a procedure.

But just then, I received a phone call from Ben's family instructing me to approve the life support. I was informed plainly that it was not up to me. It was quite clear to me that there was no room for further discussion.

Trauma

Isn't it strange that time is not always absolute but relative to what is happening to you? One minute of a fuzzy romantic moment would feel as if time has been suspended, but the same minute of waiting in anxiety can feel so much like an eternity.

The next four days that followed were undoubtedly the worst days I had ever experienced in my entire life. It was nothing close to anything I had experienced over the last seven months of his illness. It was like being locked in a nightmare and I couldn't get back out.

His frail body laid in a tangle of tubes all over him. He was hooked onto a machine with the purpose of prolonging his life, or was it prolonging the *dying process*?

The hum of the life support machine broke the deafening silence, as I stood in the room watching helplessly from the foot of his bed. I simply did not know what else I could do, except watch his life slowly being drained from him until it was completely gone.

He had several catheters and collection bags attached to his body that seemed to drain different kinds of fluid of varying colours. It was a picture that looked incredibly painful and horrific. A picture I had tried to forget every day after that.

I spent those four days, just *watching* him die, painfully and slowly. And to even think that I actually had a part in this cruel send-off made it all the more ludicrous.

It looked so much like punishing rather than rescuing him. It just seemed so utterly absurd to me. It was hard to do something when you did not understand why you were doing it. You could not see the benefit of the detriment when you were standing with a different set of beliefs that was entirely contrary to what was required of you.

So that whole unpleasant trauma consumed you until it became a part of you.

11

Finding a New Normal

After Ben's passing, my two boys and I seemed to retreat into our own little worlds, not really knowing how to go on in the first few months. We no longer had our usual weekend family day nor planned annual trips to look forward to. Even the daily dinners didn't feel quite the same as before. Everything just felt like work.

Perhaps because my children were teenage boys, I was often greeted with more awkwardness than understanding whenever I spoke about missing their father. It simply felt less painful when we just went about our own thing. Little did I know, the new adjustments and small changes that were taking place were becoming a new normal for my children and me.

Finding Work

Five months after Ben was called Home to be with the LORD, the company he was working with offered me a position in the legal department. I had not worked for many years in a regimented nine-to-five setting ever since the children came along, and waking up early had undoubtedly been the biggest challenge for me.

I remember how Ben would tiptoe around the room, not wanting to wake me as he prepared to leave for work each morning. Most of the time, he would still end up waking me slightly when he adjusted the comforter over me or planted a kiss on my face before leaving the room.

I was ecstatic at the prospect of working in the same office where my husband worked for almost two decades of his life. I excitedly took the same route and time Ben had taken to get to work. I must have walked along the same steps in the building, passed the same turnstile possibly and touched the same buttons in the lifts.

I met the same people he had worked with and had lunch at some of the same restaurants near the office where he used to frequent. Was I obsessed to the point of making others uncomfortable? I guess I would never really know even though that was certainly not what I had intended. I was simply curious to see the work life of my beloved husband, and I was not about to let any opportunity pass me by.

However, the unfamiliar pressures in my new work life soon began to overshadow the initial excitement of a possible light ahead. It began to weigh me down quickly. The supervisor at work made it clear to me from the first week that no one had trained him when he had first started work. He said he had to learn everything he knew the hard way and therefore, had no interest in teaching anyone, anything. My supervisor also made little effort to hide his disdain for me though he seemed like a nice person to everyone else. He told my colleagues he resented people like me who could get in solely through connections.

Connections? At best, knowing someone in the company and having their recommendation only offers an *opportunity*. But acquiring a degree in law or any tertiary academic achievement simply does not happen without commanding years of diligent study, the discipline of showing up and passing every examination consistently throughout. There are no shortcuts nor are there any connections which can ever substitute for that. I was appalled someone as educated as him could think that way.

I did consider that maybe things would get better if I just hung in there. Maybe the work would get familiar. If others have all started that way, surely I could too! But the rope I was trying to cling onto seemed so elusive. The only familiar helpline given to me were often these words, "You do first and I will tell you if it's right. What I want to hear is, when I say 'Jump,' you ask, how high?"

I tried to win the supervisor's trust by clearing out successfully every assigned task or file within the time frame he had given. I tried to work harder and put in more personal time to research the older files of similar work. I purchased books of related work scope to study when I was home. But no matter how hard I tried to improve or meet his expectations in the ever-growing assigned tasks, I could never seem to reach it. It was always an arm's length away. Like a tease.

Instead of things getting better over time, he began to turn up the intensity. He would not use the phone intercom when he wanted to speak to me. He would yell out my name from his room, so I had to get up from where I was, sometimes several times a day, just to find out what he wanted. He would also speak about me loudly on the phone, every so often, saying everything that he thought was wrong about me. He would leave his door wide open, so that I could hear his conversations about me from my desk.

It felt so awful. But instead of rejecting it, I received it into my spirit. I let it play over and over in my head. I did not know how to deal with the emotions from this new work life, especially the condescending behaviour, the insults and scolding that were within earshot of all my colleagues from the supervisor at work on an almost daily basis.

When sympathetic colleagues suggested to him that it was only reasonable to give me time to get familiar with the work, he replied coldly, "Only those who swim, stay." He openly told my colleagues that the company was not a place of charity.

When my colleagues told me what he had said, the word 'charity' stayed in my head even after the long and dreary workday was over. I began to grow increasingly weary, demoralised and even felt a sense of worthlessness about myself.

As soon as one part switched off, another pressure would be playing in another part of my mind. It would remind me how even the slightest of my demerits in this same place could drastically affect my husband's good name, and I simply could not afford to let that happen. My husband had been a valuable asset to the company for the past two decades and people in that industry knew him. That fear irrationally kept me from wanting others to know what I was really facing at the workplace because I kept feeling it was my fault for my limitations.

Every academic excellence or accolade I had once achieved in the past could not convince me that I was capable of facing even the most mindless task at hand. I did not realise I could be so ill-prepared to face the real world without Ben.

I remembered the 'me' who had once walked into an examination hall with three invigilators staring at one another asking each other, "Has there been a mistake? Is she the only candidate in the whole country taking criminology?" They stared at me convinced there had been a mistake as all the other subjects in law had at least two hundred candidates sitting for each paper year after year. One of them began searching frantically through the papers they had pulled from a large envelope.

"Excuse me, ma'am," I called out.

Two other male invigilators who stood behind her looked up at me. After explaining to them that I was under self-study for the optional subject, only then did they quickly settle me in. I was told I could sit anywhere, unlike the usual formal setting in which seating would be determined by a given number stated in the exam docket. They even offered me snacks when they returned from their tea break.

Then I had a thought. Maybe, anyone could have self-studied an external degree subject in nine months. But then, surely not everyone could relate to having handled all four degree subjects in the late third-trimester of her pregnancy with a three-and-a-half-year-old at home, and to graduate with Honours, too, at the end of it.

While it may be true that past glories should remain in the past, as the past is not all that we are going to have, you can't claim what you didn't actually do. And so, it is for times like this when you need to remind yourself that you were the same person, just like David did when he said, "I *can* take down Goliath. I *have* killed both the lion and the bear." [1]

All of a sudden, I found that without Ben being the shield and life planner for me, I just didn't know how to cope, much less deal with the side of ugliness that seemed to be knocking on my door every day ever since.

At the workplace, every now and then, I would come across Ben's name and signature in the older documents related to the work I was assigned to. I would have to fight back tears each time, as displaying such a weakness would not be appropriate. It felt a lot like catching a glimpse of your dad standing outside of your classroom door, peering at you with pride in his eyes, but you couldn't go to him because your teacher would not allow it.

I began to lose my appetite, skipping more and more meals. I even went to bed feeling fearful and anxious, just at the mere thought that I had to go to work again the next day. I wished so much to be able to tell Ben all that I was going through because he almost always had all the answers. I also called out to God, but it was no different than calling out to the people living up on the hill, separated by a great chasm between us.

At the same time, the problems with my in-laws would turn up now and then. There were still a lot of issues and unresolved tension between us. But I did not know how to deal with them, either. So I just kept avoiding them. I was a grown woman. Yet I had never expected I would one day be so completely terrified and

---

1 Samuel 17:36 (NIV).

paralysed by fear, even just at the sound of my phone ringing and seeing their number on it.

I kept wishing so much every day that I could disappear from the face of the earth so no one would ever find me and my children again. The world just seemed to be such a hostile and scary place without Ben.

Then a family friend advised me to try speaking to a psychiatrist whom he said had come highly recommended in his medical circle. I was, of course, hesitant about it initially. After all, mental health issues are highly stigmatised in Asian culture. Seeking help is not seen as an act of empowerment but a form of weakness and shame.

After some thought, I decided to make the appointment. After a discreet forty-five-minute consultation, I was diagnosed to be *'severely depressed with suicidal tendencies'* in the medical report. I was prescribed and recommended to be on a course of antidepressants to fix my condition.

12

Depression

"I saw the world in black and white instead of the vibrant colours and shades I knew existed."

— Katie McGarry, *Pushing the Limits*

Taking the antidepressants felt a little like being hit with a terrible hangover; like you'd just had a half-dozen shots of tequila straight from the night before—only minus thc fun part, the tequila!

I was feeling light-headed most of the time. My mouth felt dry. I had heart palpitations as though my heart was going to jump out any minute. It was quite similar to a panic attack.

I felt queasy, nauseous, drowsy and lethargic. It was a menacing feeling. Yet the dullness and numbed emotions helped, like there was an invisible glass between the others and me. This made it slightly easier to be in the unpleasant environment without really taking it all in anymore. But then, I could not feel Ben, either. After a while, the familiarity of disconnectedness actually felt quite good. It started to feel a lot like an addiction. It even began to feel uncomfortable not to stay depressed.

Depression can be so insidious. It creeps up on you slowly until you lose the ability to fight it off. You get lazy. You want to give up trying because everything is so uninteresting. You just want to sink into that mode of familiarity.

There was just so much pain inside. I kept wishing I could die because it required so much effort to live. I wished I would crack under the load, so I wouldn't have to deal with so much.

But then—reality hit me.

At best, good people could only stand from afar and sympathise while unkind people would continue to run me over because *I let them*. And I wanted neither.

> ***I began to speak positively to myself.***

I did not want to be pitied or to be continuously run down any longer. It was a moment where I finally came to myself. I decided to make some *'No'* affirmations for myself. I needed to rise up and reclaim.

"NO!" I cried out.

"I simply *refuse* to go on like this! I am *not* charity, as he had said! The only thing that is lacking is a learning opportunity. Not my ability or my qualifications for the position." And almost immediately, an internal strength began to rise from within.

"Therefore, I am NOT worthless. I carry a great potential to succeed in this place. I have everything it takes to get there, in this same place as my supervisor, and he is threatened by it."

I began to speak positively to myself. I encouraged myself as David did in his great distress when there was no one else around to encourage him. The Scripture said that even when David's own people spoke of stoning him because each one was bitter in spirit towards him, but David found strength in the LORD his God.[1]

I rose up and began to speak to myself, *"I am as resilient and as tough as a nail. I am not going to die or go mad no matter how much I wish. God will not lead me so far out here—only to abandon me! None of it—is going to happen!"*

---

1 1 Samuel 30:6 (NIV).

I also decided I would no longer keep my appointment with the psychiatrist for any more follow-up medication. If kicking the pills would mean I could not cope with the conditions at the workplace, then I was clearly in the wrong place.

No one could continue to make me feel the way I did without my permission. I learned that if I don't like where I am, I am only a choice away from being somewhere else. As Maya Angelou said, "You may not control all the events that happen to you, but you can decide not to be reduced by them."

When you are in the shadows of depression, you can't see very far. It's okay even if the greatest goal is simply to get through the day. The point is not about being slow in progress, but the fact that *effort* is being made. Many tiny efforts will eventually bring about a substantial change.

Simply know that whether it is in grief or fighting depression, it is a long road ahead—but *keep walking.*

13

Prayer

"I pray because I can't help myself. I pray because I'm helpless. I pray because the need flows out of me all the time, waking and sleeping. It doesn't change God. It changes me."

—C. S. Lewis

In retrospect, it was the difficult job environment that had set me on a prayer routine. As I stepped into my car to go to work each morning, my state of inadequacy drove me into the prayer chamber. The reality of God's omnipresence assures me that God is present everywhere throughout His creation. He can hear prayers no matter where I am, whether I am in a car or even if I was in the belly of a fish like Jonah.[1]

I soon found work again in an aviation company after a good interval of rest. This time, everything was different from the last. I liked my boss, my new work environment and even the work. Best of all, I could be myself. I relished the fact I could afford to make my own mistakes and build my own merits. I could live out of my husband's shadow. No one would treat me differently, whether it was nicer or harsher, just because I was related to Ben.

Perhaps my superior at work often sensed my lack of confidence despite my enthusiasm to learn. One day he called me

1 Jonah 2:1 (NIV).

in and said this to me. "If you remain passionate about your work and are willing to learn, there is no end to learning. We can all learn together. Take your time and enjoy the process. I'll say, in five years, you will know enough to be running a department of your own."

Five years? I thought I was expected to know everything and more the day I landed the job! Perhaps it was good I went through such a rough beginning, after all. Everything that was difficult soon became rewarding when I got better at it. The more I learned, the less I took for granted.

The Bitter Water

Like Naomi the widow, my water that was once sweet had turned bitter. In Ruth 1:20, she told them, "Don't call me Naomi. Call me Mara, because the Almighty has made my life very bitter." In the same manner as Naomi, I could make a choice to either stay bitter or trust the Almighty that my water will turn sweet again.

I realised I could never be totally free to move on if I chose to remain tied to the cords of my past. I could never go the distance if I still remained adamant in carrying the burden of the past injustices and offenses with me.

I could never go the distance if I still remained adamant in carrying the burdens of the past injustices and offenses with me.

So one morning, I began by going through a few names and praying aloud I would forgive so and so. But I wasn't fully convinced I really did because it still felt the same. It was simply an intellectual decision I had made because I no longer wished to carry the weight of unforgiveness with me.

And then I felt a tug in my heart like God was saying, "Pray for them and bless them now." I struggled a little when I tried.

I found that the stronger the degree of hate that I had towards someone, the greater the degree of challenge it was for me to bless. But as I began to bless each person who had in the past left a bitter taste in my mouth, I began to immediately feel a release and such peace as I had not felt in a long time.

I realised it was really for my own good when I forgave others. My spirit was restored to health and wellness once again. I learned that I could be a hundred percent right, yet holding onto the offences would only rob me of my joy and strength. All of a sudden, I simply understood it was for my own protection and benefit when I chose to bless others and let them go.

Then I heard the LORD say, "Now pray and ask for their salvation."

This time, I felt a stronger resistance. The problem was—I didn't want it to happen for them. I began to reason with God, "I can't understand how Heaven can be a happy place if there are people there who can continue to hurt us!"

And I felt the silence of God in the space that I was in; like a light had been turned off in the room, and I was there in the dark again.

Surrender

I struggled for some time but eventually broke through. As I began to release one name after another to the LORD, my spiritual sight was being restored once again.

In the light of His love, I became convinced of my own immaturity towards every one of them. I began to feel compassion when the LORD enabled me to see things from their perspective. I began to ask God to forgive *me* as I repented of my own transgressions towards Him.

I prayed and asked that God would grant each one salvation for their souls, just as I had been prompted to do. This time, I asked with a clean heart and a simple child-like faith. No longer questioning anything but simply in obedience and quiet trust to see the good with my heart—and not with my eyes.

I learned that I could still trust God even though I did not have to understand everything. Even though nothing unusual happened after praying, I felt a reassuring peace in my heart; like God was over the water and everything was going to be all right.

Then some weeks later, I began to feel a strange prompting to phone Ben's father. It had been at least four years since we last met or spoke since Ben's passing. He was very much a reticent person. A man of few words, yet everyone knew he cared about each member of the family in the most genuine and personal way. Though he might not express his emotions in words, he would often display his love and compassion quietly through his actions.

I remember in the early years when he was healthier and still moving about, he would buy breakfast and groceries for the family. Whenever we went back to Melaka during weekends, he would make a special stop to get me my favourite *tang-hoon* (glass noodles) fish ball soup on the way back to the family house, even though I had not requested it.

I always felt moved each time I woke up to the packet of noodles on the kitchen table because I knew my father-in-law had made the effort to do something nice for me. His gesture assured me that I was included in his thoughts as being one of their own. The parking for that particular stall had always been challenging, especially during weekends. I imagined the inconvenience that even I would not go through for myself. Not only that, he would even instruct the lady to hold the pepper because he knew that I liked my food better without it. Though he had never articulated his emotions towards us, I felt cared for and accepted.

Aside from our usual greetings and courteous niceties, we barely ever had conversations. It had always been that way since the day I became a member of their family. So what was I going to say if I called him? So much had happened between us in that period when Ben was sick. I fought with the feeling for quite a while.

I thought of Ben and how pleased he would be, if I did make the call. Since it was close to the Lunar New Year, at least I would have a few greeting lines to get us through the first minute or so. And maybe, that was all we needed.

I took a long deep breath and began to dial his number. When his voice came on the phone, I proceeded with the greetings as light-hearted as I had planned.

So far, so good.

But what he said next was totally unexpected. He asked, "Are you well? When are you coming home?"

I was momentarily stunned as I had not expected that I would still be wanted in their home because their son had died. I had anticipated that he must have missed his grandsons very much, yet it was not about them that he asked, but *me*.

After some awkward silence, I promised him that I would visit one day with his grandchildren. As we both hung up, it felt strange for a while. The heaviness in my heart was gone and my spirit felt lighter.

Two more years passed before I gathered enough courage to call Ben's mother this time. It had been a little over six years since we had met or spoken to each other. I vividly remember the last time was at the hospital, the day that Ben died.

The coldness between us broke after a few moments of tense silence. In that brief call over the phone that afternoon, I was glad that we had the opportunity to make our peace with each other. I was actually happy to know that she, too, had accepted Jesus as her Saviour in recent years.

I realised that I no longer feared the same things I did when I became willing to let go and let God take the lead. When I took the step to recognise my own pride and repent of it, I set myself right with God again. When I forgive, release and let go—my heart becomes free to love and celebrate others once more.

Forgiveness

Forgiveness, as I have discovered, is a journey just like grief. It is a journey because it is a concerted and conscious effort that one has to put in daily. I sleep with the choice that I have made the night before that I was going to forgive someone. I wake up in the morning and I have to make a conscious choice to forgive again because I still feel the same hurt.

As Randall Worley once said, "Forgiveness is not an emotion, it's a decision." It has nothing to do with how much knowledge you have. Life either expands or contracts in direct proportion to your willingness to forgive.

When we forgive, we return to God the right to take care of justice. We relinquish our right to hurt them *even if* we could. I have heard it said before that it is, in effect, saying "Forgiveness means: I am giving up my right to hurt you for hurting me."

Forgiveness is simply a creative act that changes us from prisoners of the past to liberated people at peace with our memories. It is *not* forgetfulness. It is simply an act of surrender for better things to come into our lives. Life is lived at its best when we travel light!

14

Change Is Never Easy

"Change is never easy, you fight to hold on, and you fight to let go."

—Mareez Reyes

Have you ever awakened to a supremely lovely morning, yet simply felt like something was missing?

Imagine you have just been given a new and beautiful kite to fly. Yet the height in which it could soar in the glorious open skies is limited because you do not allow yourself to release more line than what you believe is comfortable. Each time it catches the wind, the kite would take off higher and further away. Though the thrill and exhilaration of being free would set in, so would the unsettling insecurity. So you tug it and reel it back in, keeping the line close.

As Marilyn Ferguson said, "It's not so much that we're afraid of change or so in love with the old ways, but it's that place in between that we fear … It's like between trapezes. It's Linus when his blanket is in the dryer. There's nothing to hold on to." Perhaps true to what H. L. Mencken made in his observations in his book *Minority Report* in 1956, "most people want security in this world, not liberty."

Even though I was now free to make my own decisions, I still made most of them based on what I believed Ben would have approved of—instead of what I really wanted, simply because it felt safer that way.

My Solo Travel

When Ben was undergoing his chemotherapy, we made plans that when he recovered, we would go to Europe together. Towards the last bit of his battle with cancer, he told me, "If I don't make it … you go."

And I asked him, "But … but, how can I go without you?" He looked into my eyes and replied, "Why not?"

What he said that afternoon in the hospital room has come back to me many times. It challenged my own limitations through the years, thereafter. I was so dependent on him in planning everything for me that I was too afraid to even try imagining a life without him in it. Yet his absence had become my reality.

Nancy Stephan once said, "There are things that we don't want to happen but have to accept, things we don't want to know but have to learn, and people we can't live without but have to let go."

Three and a half years after Ben's passing, I decided to challenge myself in doing things I never thought I would have the courage to do and visit places I would never dare to go. *Alone.*

In essence, I just wanted to prove, by silencing my own critic, that I was capable of living life on my own and to become so much more. So I got my flight tickets, and the adventure in Europe began in the summer of 2011.

I wasn't sure what to expect. Nor did I have a real itinerary up my sleeves. As crazy as it sounds, I knew that it was just something I had to do for myself. Others' opinion of me mattered little, and I found that liberating. When you feel dead inside, you truly care very little about dying or anything else. And maybe it was for that reason I was doing it because I needed to learn how to live again.

I passed through country after country. All throughout the journey, I walked around—city after city, towns and counties. I met more people than I'd ever encountered in all my years alive. Places where I had friends, I was able to enjoy their generous hospitality. Places where I didn't know anyone, I relied on the local tours and making new friends along the way.

I took planes, trains and buses by myself to places I had never been. I was surprised to have been met with more kindness out there than I ever expected to find back home. I remember the most heart-warming encounters during that period were not with people I knew, but were with those at random with total strangers.

One thing is true. We will never know how much courage we have until we are afraid. And courage is simply the ability to embrace something that is much bigger than yourself and to find that when up close, fear—when confronted—isn't as big or as formidable as what you believe it to be.

In *David and Goliath: Underdogs, Misfits, and the Art of Battling Giants*, Malcolm Gladwell writes:

> What the Israelites saw from high on the ridge was an intimidating giant. In reality, the very thing that gave the giant his size was also the source of his greatest weakness. There is an important lesson in that for battles with all kinds of giants. The powerful and the strong are not always what they seem.

Bus Stop

It was a cold morning in Southend, and I was going to London that day. There was an elderly gentleman already at the bus stop. We exchanged a smile and a nod. It didn't take long before he asked where I was going. After a courteous exchange of small talk, I asked him the same thing.

My room in the quiet valley of Lauterbrunnen, Switzerland

I learned that his wife had passed away two years prior, and ever since, he would make a two-hour trip to their lovely country cottage. He would stay there for a fortnight and spend the time painting. He even showed me an unfinished piece that he had been working on.

It was a beautiful oil painting of scenery that was set against a backdrop of the lush native landscape of the cottage where he was staying. They didn't have children and painting helped him cope with his loss and loneliness, he said. There was a silent connection between us, as we both stared at that painting. Maybe, it was empathy.

I told him about Ben—that it had been three years for me—and how I was *still* pining for him. There was a look in his eyes, like we had both converged on the same note of pain.

Soon, his bus arrived. I will never forget the sight of him waving back at me from the bus window. There was so much sweetness about him and at the same time, sadness and loneliness, too.

Henry Wadsworth Longfellow once said, "Ships that pass in the night, and speak each other in passing, only a signal shown, and a distant voice in the darkness; So on the ocean of life, we pass and speak one another, only a look and a voice, then darkness again and a silence."

The moment that we get will always only be in the *now*. Once it passes, every encounter will disappear into the vastness of the huge ocean of life once again. And I will always be glad that I was present at that particular moment, sharing a smile or a kind word that might mean nothing, or perhaps everything, to another lonely soul.

After spending months away alone, crossing oceans and continents, I learned something very important. And that is, whether I was standing at the peak of the Grand Alpine of the Swiss Alps, or being wooed by the romance of Italy or the vineyards in France, I found that my pain followed me wherever

I went. It was the same whether I was on the other side of the globe, or if I was right at home. I just could *never* stop thinking about Ben.

I could not run away from my own pain, even though I liked the rhythm of the open road and changing landscapes beckoning me on the horizon. Even in the midst of such a breathtakingly spectacular landscape, where I was overlooking it all, his absence had the power to obliterate everything in a heartbeat. Nothing makes you lonelier than seeing a beautiful sunrise or a stunning sunset *alone* when you are in grief, thousands of miles away from home.

His absence had the power to obliterate everything in a heartbeat.

After passing through the ninth country, I was actually excited to be heading home and discovered what was to be the best part of my whole solo adventure. I found that apart from the comfort of seeing my children again, nothing quite beats being in my own bed after months of being away! A value that would *never* have had as much appeal had I never left.

15

Loneliness

"Our language has wisely sensed the two sides of being alone. It has created the word "loneliness" to express the pain of being alone. And it has created the word "solitude" to express the glory of being alone."

—Paul Johannes Tillich

One day, I sat alone watching the rain patter dismally on my windowsill. The smell and sound of rain that I used to love induced a pain I did not wish to resist, nor did I want it to stay. After the shower, the whole earth felt so clean and refreshed. It was as if yesterday's troubles were all washed away and everything became new again. I caught a renewed breath of air in my lungs. I looked up to see the tiny, dazzling, diamond droplets as they sat resting and shimmering atop the fir needles. It was absolutely resplendent. But then, the sharp sense of loneliness engulfed me once again.

Social Life

The family relations and friends, whom I had liberally called mine all this time, were really Ben's family relations and friends. Only now, I realised that it's not the same thing.

I remember dreading every single invitation that came after his passing. Some I could avoid, some not. Every function or gathering that I had to attend without him was harder than I could anticipate. Being introverted makes it even harder for others to truly understand. The thought of having to drive myself to an unfamiliar dinner location or walk into a room full of people without him was enough to send me into a sudden panic attack more times than I could remember. The time that I looked forward to most was usually when it ended.

Being Alone

I wasn't sure what bothered me more—being alone or being lonely. It was often when I was alone that I felt extremely lonely. I was lonely, yet I dreaded being invited to gatherings where happy people congregated. I did not enjoy the feeling that I had to work extra hard to 'blend in' so as not to ruin it for others, or being made to feel like a social misfit or a killjoy if I didn't.

Family and friends would always cut me off almost immediately to that 'alone' line as soon as I say it. They would never fail to remind me, "But, *at least*—you still have your children. And you have two of them!"

I am *quite* certain I can handle the simple arithmetic of the number of children that I have, even with the frequent bouts of amnesia, yet I could not help but feel minimized whenever the 'at least' phrases were being uttered. Why do most people around us naturally assume that our children can simply replace a spouse and that life will go back to being 'normal' just as it did before?

Children are such precious gifts we are entrusted to be responsible for. Some are more mature and sweeter than others. They are able to make your life and work a breeze; whilst some, on the other hand may simply need more love, attention and prayers. Either way, we just have to be there for them when they need us. Period.

But, they are *not* our equals. We simply cannot hold the same intimate aspirations or relate in the same manner as we would with a spouse, or even with another adult who isn't our spouse.

When Does the Shadow of Grief End?

I searched the web for years eager to know when I would start feeling better again. Some medical websites I had visited seemed to suggest six months, while some maintained it was up to two years. After crossing the second-year milestone and not a bit better than the first six months, my thoughts only grew darker from then on.

I couldn't seem to pull away from the melancholy that was always following me around. Every prayer I made to God seemed to be in the same eloquence, wrapped around the familiar lines that had found its way from beneath the shallow shell of my being. It was like a persistent restless child, tugging at the hem of mother's dress and always asking, "When am I going to see Ben? How much longer? Are we close? Are we even close yet?"

There had been days when the birds were singing. The air was cool and crisp with the smell and aroma of coffee wafting in the air. The blooms were glorious and I thought I had just stepped right into heaven! Everything was in place. No sick kids. The happy housekeeper was as chirpy as a singing bird. A tune would come into my head: *everything is beautiful ... in its own way ...*

Then, next thing I know, a wave of sadness would crash over me. I would be so bewildered by an unexpected thought that had seemed to come from nowhere: *Great. Now I can go kill myself.*

That even on a day most perfect, when everything seemed to be well placed, the deep sense of void could seem so totally unbearable. There was both an active atrophy and an ebullient, zestful resilience both at war behind this facade. I yearned for a change, yet I simply could not find the door out of a dark room.

16

The Source of Light

"God is light; in him there is no darkness at all."

—1 John 1:5

Some new friends I made from the church close to where I lived invited me to join their church camp. It was on the second day at the camp when I kept seeing the same picture in my mind during the worship service. I learned later that it was known as a 'vision'. God can use many ways to communicate His direction to people today, just as He did in the days of creation.

As my eyes were shut, focused in a quiet prayerful mode, the imagery in my mind's eye began to open up. I saw myself sitting on a bench under this huge and solid, sheltering, oak-like tree. I knew that it must be a good picture because I saw radiance and light that surrounded me. I saw a green and expansive field that was stretched out onto the horizon right before me. I had an uncanny sense of *knowing* that the field represented my work or life assignments ahead. I could not see what was in the field, or the details in it, because the light was so bright that it was almost blinding. Even though it was a beautiful picture, there was a sense of loneliness that I felt about it.

I began asking God in the most ineloquent and brazen way, arising out of desperation, as well as exasperation, *"WHERE ARE YOU, GOD? Do You even know what I need?"* I waited, but sensed only silence.

I perceived for a moment that perhaps He really *didn't.* After all, I have been familiar with the male presence in my life, as they were often clueless when it came to the delicate complexities of the emotions of a female.

So I revealed it outright, "I NEED A HUG, GOD! Can ***You*** *hug me, God?*"

I felt a deep sense of despair at what I had just requested in my heart. How could God, who is *Spirit,* hug me? What was I even thinking? (Or not!) Such total absurdity!

Then through the loud speakers, I heard an invitation for those who would like to be prayed for to go up to the front. My desperation for a divine intervention of a change in my life drew me to the front of the altar that day.

Every second of waiting in line for my turn to be prayed for was another second where I heard the voice in my head telling me to turn back. *"Go back to your seat, it's pointless,"* it said. Finally, it was my turn.

The leaders asked me, "What would you like us to pray for you?" I paused for a few seconds and I thought to myself, *This is just great.* I couldn't possibly tell them I would like a hug from God! What would they even think?

I had been so distracted with trying to fight off the earlier thought of going back to my seat, I did not realise how my prayer request would actually sound until that moment when I had to make it known.

As the leaders waited, I quickly thought of another prayer request that would sound more normal. So I told them I had made a recent application to the UN as a voluntary legal assistant just a week earlier and asked if they would pray for me. We then closed our eyes. I heard one of the leaders begin praying I would have peace to know if the job would be right for me. Then she stopped.

I thought, *Okay, so that was a really short prayer.* Just the kind I would like said before meals. I waited for her cue to end the prayer but then after a short pause, she continued, "I sense that Father God wants to give you a hug."

That line shook me like a thunderbolt. I was clearly not expecting that at all. And as she reached over and put her arms around me, I began to cry like a little child in the embrace of a warm body.

I had grown so disconnected to the idea of God and religion, I no longer knew what I truly believed anymore. Lewis writes in *A Grief Observed* " … don't talk to me about the consolations of religion or I shall suspect that you don't understand." He was a faithful clergy, a man of faith. Yet grief is a powerful force that knocks even the mightiest men and women overboard.

I had never verbalised my need for a hug to another soul except through the muted cries expressed from my heart just moments ago. And it was also, in a manner that was raw, defiant and disrespectful. But obviously, God is far more merciful than what many seem to depict of Him. God is not a religion, but a triune divine Person. He can hear us when we cry out to Him. And He can reveal His love to those who are willing to come to a place of truthfulness, even if one comes angry, yelling and kicking.

He can hear us when we cry out to Him.

As I walked back to my seat, I felt a great sense of peace and comfort. When I closed my eyes, the picture of me sitting on a bench under the magnificent sheltering tree appeared once again in my mind.

But this time, I felt a prompting to look at the mental picture from both sides of where I was sitting. My peripheral vision in my mind had always been limited because I only chose to see it from the same angle every time.

As I turned my head to the other side, I saw someone else with me on the bench. Tears welled up in my eyes as I looked at Him. *"LORD!"* I called out. "You have been here with me all this time?"[1]

In a simple mental picture, I saw that it was my own stubbornness all along that had kept me from seeing the whole picture. If only I was willing to look at the circumstances of my life from a different *angle*, I would have been able to live it with a different *perspective*. That is, I had *never* been truly alone.

---

1 Psalm 16:8 (NIV). I know that the LORD is always with me. I will not be shaken because He is right beside me.

17

That Awkward Age

"I've learned that you shouldn't go through life with a catcher's mitt on both hands; you need to be able to throw something back."

—Maya Angelou

I used to think that turning 12 was an awkward age until I got to be 13. And it never felt any different ever since.

Being widowed at 39 meant that as a healthy, normal woman, I still longed to be romanced, had sexual urges as well as desires, and most importantly, had the need to be noticed, admired and loved. I wished that expression was possible with the spouse who I had loved more than life itself but, alas, life's plan does not always turn out the way we like it to be.

I had the closest encounter with my dentist when I went in for an annual dental check with my two boys one afternoon. He was, as always, donned in a white coat, surgical half-face mask and those white latex gloves. He was of a medium frame in his early 40s. He wore glasses but he was cute. Behind it was a pair of smiling eyes.

While reclining trustingly in the dental chair, I felt a momentary rush of adrenaline as he bent closer to my face in order to examine the more hidden parts of my cavities. I could also hear the sound of the screeching drill in his hand. In the blinding light just above him, I couldn't see his face except to notice this was a real person who was soft spoken with a kind soothing voice.

I could feel a part of his hand resting on my face. It had been so long since anyone had touched my face that it felt rather good, despite the hint of a strong unpleasant latex smell. He had a calm and confident composure about him that simply put me at ease.

After it was all done, I got up from the chair. And just as I was about to get to the door, he called out to me, "Hey, see you again—(pause) next year!"

I turned my head towards him where our eyes met from a distance. My fingers were already wrapped around the doorknob and I was just about ready to step out. I gave him a polite nod and flashed across the dentist-approved smile. I replied, perhaps a little too enthusiastically, with one of my shoulders up and head tilted slightly, "Okay, can't wait!"

It felt so weird when I caught myself flirting! I shook my head but laughed out a little at the silliness of what had just taken place in the playground of my mind. For a brief moment, I envied the woman who was his wife, whoever she was. I imagined him returning to a welcoming home with a lovely wife and happy children at the end of every evening, just like the one I used to know. For a brief moment, I wished I had one I could go back to again.

Since Ben's passing, I had to reinvent and redefine new meaning to everything that was once familiar to me. What is day or night, weekend or not? What does it matter? They remained to me like muted inconsequential seconds and minutes of time that was quickly slipping by me.

18

Dating

"The weeping widow lives up to our expectations.
The widow who dances and dates does not."

—Sheryl Sandberg, *Option B*

When a spouse dies, biological needs, unfortunately, do not. Yet much guilt surrounds these needs, as if the surviving spouse would be more noble if it did not.

I remember being angry with God. I kept praying and asking God to remove and take away every desire that was sexual in me because I did not wish to sin against Him. But I simply could not pray it away. The more I prayed and resisted it, the greater the temptation appeared to be.

The world convinces us that what *feels* good *is* good. In pain, we look for ways to escape into a world where we often seek comfort in the wrong places. Suggestive images and downright sexually explicit material bombard us from every corner, even when we aren't looking for it. Entertain it for a minute and it defiles something inside of us, creating a bigger hole of isolation and frustration.

The needs are real, yet the answers aren't always available or clear because they are coloured by the values held by people around us. Even then, it isn't something a widow can talk about without being judged more harshly compared to our counterparts.

To know I must not 'cross the line' was simply not enough. The more my fear of God increased, the more I cared about God's feelings. By *fear*, I do not mean compelled intimidation to observe the laws of religion. Rather, I care about not hurting someone I love because how that person feels matters to me.

As I became more aware that I hurt God when I sin, the revelation of His grace became strength for me to turn around and run. Sin hurts God because it hurts *me*. When I understood that sexual purity is important because it is meant to protect me physically, emotionally and spiritually, I was able to appreciate the value in walking away from unhealthy relationships or environments that could lead me into it.

***Sin hurts God because it hurts* me.**

It took a long while before the word 'widow' finally registered in my head and that the category actually includes *me*! 'Widow' was a word that I couldn't even bring myself to utter, even though that is what a married woman whose husband has died is known as.

Widowhood comes with a stigma that separates you from the married to another category of the obsolete. You get looked at in a funny way and are treated differently because of it. You feel less than, compared to your married relatives and friends, *even if* their marriage screams 'on the rocks'.

As one who had tasted the sweet nectar of love, it was only natural to wish for the winter in my heart to experience warmth once again. Probably the hardest bit of my life experience is, at 20, I got to choose whomever I wanted. After 40, I could only *hope* to even get noticed by someone I could remotely imagine a future with.

As someone said, dating after 40 is like being thrown into a serial killer's basement, while others may agree that it feels like you have just stepped into the list of some dating clearinghouse. And some horrible dates do validate that feeling, unfortunately.

Aikido-Mate

Sometimes, when I was bored out of my wits being home alone on a Saturday evening, I did wish dating were as easy as going out with the opposite sex as long as he had a pulse. Unfortunately, those with qualities which I had long admired were either married, gay or dead.

Slightly after two years of Ben's passing, I signed up for a self-defence class in Aikido. I remember sustaining a broken toenail on the first day of training in this martial art. I never knew there was a right way to fall when someone pushes you off balance or throws you down.

I couldn't even count the number of falls that often left me with bruises from the training sessions ever since I started. I was just relieved to have my skull still perfectly intact after several months into it. I couldn't say I knew of anyone who had ever died in practice, as I did not stick around long enough to find out.

In Aikido, everyone, whether male or female, gets equal practice time in class to be flipped or thrown over and over again onto the thinly cushioned mat. A quick position to bounce back immediately is expected.

You weren't allowed to just lie there like a dead dog—even if it might have felt or sounded like we had just been thrown off a cliff and landed on the rocks. A senior fellow student once explained to me that, similarly in life, we are to carry the same concept that when we are down, we must get up quickly. Makes good sense.

Soon, I could not help but notice that one of the senior trainees in my class seemed somewhat interested in me. But then again, I could be wrong. His shy and quiet demeanour seemed to have attracted me to him, too. We found ourselves drawn to each other as practice partners week after week.

Even though we had met each other regularly in training, we had not exchanged more than ten sentences put together during that time. So when he asked if I wanted to meet him for lunch one day, I didn't even wait two seconds to answer, "Yes!" We agreed to meet later that week.

On the day of the date, I chose a nice dress to put on. It felt slightly strange, but I was a little excited at the same time. I felt like a teenager being asked out on a date *(a long time ago).*

I arrived early at the restaurant. I chose a seat in a slightly hidden and most nondescript corner I could find with my back to the entrance. I did not wish for anyone to see me there on a date.

I was jittery the whole time. I wasn't sure if it was because I felt guilty for being disloyal to Ben, or if I was simply afraid of being judged by someone who knew me if they spotted me there.

While waiting, I took off my wedding ring and put it in my purse. I was determined to do what normal 'single-again' people do: have coffee, eat, chat and get to know each other without ever feeling like the ghost of my deceased spouse was going to judge me for accepting another. Who knows, this could be the beginning of a beautiful friendship, and maybe, even a serious relationship sometime in the future?

I began to daydream a little. I thought of the activities and places we could go if we were in a relationship. I daydreamed of having someone walk beside me—not just in the physical sense, but also for the remainder of my life's journey.

The lunch started well. It was, on the whole, pleasant for about the first half hour, until something he said felt like a handful of gravel in my mouth. It was no different had I been chewing on cardboard for the rest of the lunch.

When I got back to my car, I searched for the ring in my purse and slipped it back on. I felt so very foolish. The one most important question I had forgotten to ask before accepting the lunch date was his MARITAL STATUS!

Why did I even assume he was not married when he had asked me out? Was it because I had never, even once, seen him with a wedding band? And why wasn't he wearing it? Perhaps he didn't like jewellery. Even then, couldn't he have, at the very least, made it known before the lunch date? Come to think of it, why did he even ask me out alone if he was a married person? Shouldn't there be a law somewhere for that? Oh, I don't know—death penalty, or something close?

As I drove out of the parking bay, I couldn't help but think of Ben. He would have smashed my date into a bloody pulp for what I had just put myself through!

Self-Worth

In widowhood, we grapple with the initial loss and eventually step into the reality of coping and managing life without our other half. We learn to adapt. No one who isn't in our shoes can ever hear the silence we often describe as deafening or the loneliness that feels as parched as the wilderness.

The world of widowhood is forever silent of compliments and generous thoughts from a loving spouse who notices *you*. One of the toughest battles in the war of loss is to wean off the need for validation in order to feel I am worth something. People say time heals and makes everything all right. *No, it doesn't.* Time simply creates a distance that takes you further from the physical reality of your loved ones and, thus, reduces the extreme intensity of grief through the passage of time.

I had to learn to be okay, so that if I were never given another compliment or approval from anyone again, it would still *not* diminish the value I carry in my life. The sympathy of others can only accompany us for a short distance. Once you have overrun it, people can be incredibly hurtful even when they mean well. But then, I learned the truth about God's love is that we can *never* exhaust it.

In *A Grief Observed*, C.S. Lewis said, "An odd by-product of my loss is that I'm aware of being an embarrassment to everyone I meet. Perhaps the bereaved ought to be isolated in special settlements like lepers." The thing about widowhood is, I could sense the awkwardness my coupled friends have when they are with me. I could not help but feel quite terribly out of place, too. That sense of alienation doesn't go away easily, despite the best efforts of your friends, or even yourself.

It was the identity vacuum that startled me since the wake of grief. Would my self-worth diminish just because my status had changed from being a wife to being a widow? Would it now become devalued simply because I had aged?

The young woman in her 20s when she met her true love is still inside me. Her passions, her ambitions and her capacity to love and be loved; she is still there. Though I still feel the same young spirit inside on most days, the tyranny of the mirror often does not do justice in reflecting the inner person we still are.

Status, or even beauty, has been defined in so many ways. If I were to look to the approval of the world and be judged by its ever-changing standards, then the feelings of self-pity are not baseless. But thankfully, God has a different standard than that of the world. Even though I cannot defy gravity to stop aging, I can stop allowing the culture of youth and beauty define my worth.

I once heard of an illustration of a coin that fell into the mud. The things that had happened to the coin did nothing to change the value it held. If it was a denomination carrying the value of a dollar, it is still a dollar next to a new, clean coin.

Therefore, when my self-worth is anchored in what my Creator thinks of me, rather than from people or possessions, then my value does not decrease simply because someone else does not have the ability to see my worth.

19

Soul Tie

"One keeps on emerging from a phase, but it always recurs. Round and round. Everything repeats ..."

—C.S. Lewis, *A Grief Observed*

I was in bed one night listening to Pastor Mike Connell teaching on the subject of soul ties on YouTube.[1] As he spoke, my mind began to open up to a scene where I had walked up to Ben's bedside in the Intensive Care Unit. I was reminded of that afternoon in which I had given a promise to my dying spouse.

I remember telling Ben that I was giving him permission to let go as I could not bear to see him suffer in pain any longer. I gave him my assurance that he did not have to worry about our children as I will care for them, and a vow that would keep me bound for the duration of the promise when I uttered these words to him, "I will love you *forever*, Ben."

Ben was in a deeply sedated state at that time. I learned later that it didn't matter if he had heard it or not because *words are powerful.* Once released into the atmosphere, they carry an energy that is binding until a severance is made.

---

1 Mike Connell, "Breaking Free from Unhealthy Attachments," July 19, 2016, https://www.youtube.com/watch?v=pFIyetcsdN8

For years and years, the pain still felt so raw—like everything had just taken place only yesterday. I felt continually sad, even long after the time of healthy grieving, but I simply didn't understand why. No matter how hard I tried to work on feeling better, it was always like taking one step forward but two steps back. It was not only exhausting but incredibly frustrating as well.

Someone said that hanging onto a dead past is like trying to keep afloat with weights tied to our ankles. What I thought was loyalty and faithfulness to a promise which was no longer demanded of me had, in fact, held me captive to a prison within myself. It was as if I was always fighting a force that kept pulling me backwards each time I tried to advance forward.

Then I heard something Pastor Mike said from the sermon that captured my attention. "Attachments that were once good can become destructive when we hold them tightly to ourselves when the season for the purpose had ended." His words kept resonating in my mind. It was like echoes reverberating in my head.

My heart lay open before the LORD that night. I saw Ben as the place of nurture for which I had been unwilling to let go. I had once depended on him for love, providence, security, approval, admiration and validation, as well as comfort. I had loved him with the whole of my being. Though he was my husband, he *belonged* to God.

My fear of losing Ben completely, even though he had been reduced to only a memory, was still very much a terrifying thought. How do you let go of what used to make so much sense, while everything ahead seems like a blur?

But right there, I was beginning to see the picture. If I only had my vision set on the remnants of yesterday, I would not be able to enjoy the abundance that I still have ahead of me.

Convinced that God could still lead me from the wilderness into a land of promise, I clasped my hands together and began to pray aloud. Arresting every molecule, every ion and particle, subduing it by the prayer made to the One who created it all.

I cried out, *"Father, I cut off this soul tie to my dead husband, Ben, right now, in JESUS' name! Amen!"*

Released

There was no lightning or peals of thunder to mark that moment. But I could instantly feel *something* had changed. As soon as I had released those words by making my choice clear, the weight of pain, like a kind of deep sorrow which had been tied to the back of my heart, obeyed and *left*. However, I did not tell anyone immediately because I wanted to be sure I was not simply imagining the relief.

The next morning when I woke up, I searched for that familiar attachment of pain. And I was aware that the pain and heaviness were no longer there. It felt similar to an empty pocket of air in that same space that used to hold the weight of pain.

I told my son Edwin that I felt like going out to enjoy a really nice meal that day. I felt strangely *happy*, and I even had a desire to *celebrate*. He appeared somewhat stunned as I related to him the simple prayer I prayed just the night before. Who could have believed that all it took was a simple prayer of faith to help me regain an emotion which I had lost for the past nine years since his father's passing?

I walked out into the garden. It was a lovely afternoon. I felt the warmth of the sun on my face. I began to inhale deeply. The scent of freshly cut grass and flowers in the air was invigorating. Even the blooms in the garden appeared strangely more vibrant and alive than ever before. Have they always looked that way? The familiar dull and nagging ache of loneliness that used to accompany me seemed to have vacated, too.

I began to experience more and more moments of blissful solitude when I actually enjoyed being alone, but *not* being lonely.

20

Legacy

"A good name is more desirable than great riches, a good reputation is better than silver and gold."

—Proverbs 22:1

Both my parents were early Chinese immigrants who travelled to South East Asia, attracted by the prospect of work and opportunities in business. They eventually settled in Melaka, a port city famed for its spice trade through the strategic Straits. My family lived in one of those pre-war shop houses that still stand today. In the early architectural designs of those days, we even had our own water well that was centrally located in the courtyard where water was drawn for washing. Adjacent to it sat the humble kitchen where family meals were prepared. My childhood home held many memories for me that echoes of a distant past.

I remember as a child, it used to be quite unnerving to get to the bedrooms on the first floor, as the stairway was poorly lit and the wooden stairs creaked beneath our bare feet as we climbed. I would wait up for my parents to retire for the night, so I did not have to be alone upstairs during bedtime.

Being the youngest in the family, the most vivid memory I had of my father was that he used to help me with my schoolwork. Not only that, he used to piggyback me to our room whenever I fell asleep while waiting for my parents in the family hall downstairs.

My father passed away from pancreatic cancer when I was 12. Even though I have very little memory of my father, the picture of him carrying me on his back has quite comfortably helped me understand the concept of God as *my Father*. I became a Christian not long after he died.

When it was time for my children to grapple with their own grief, I could only pray the tender years they had spent with their father would be enough to sustain them through times when I was inadequate for being the sole parent left for them.

Memories

In retrospect, I was glad to have kept a photo journal of my children since the first day they were born. Those days before digital photography took the world by storm, I would invest in a roll of Fuji or Kodak film every month. The candid shots often turned out the best because it was similar to capturing and freezing a spontaneous ordinary moment of life, itself.

Looking back at all the old pictures, it felt like only yesterday that I was nursing scraped knees, seeing them through their first days at school, celebrating their birthdays and going on holidays with Ben. Every expression, those funny faces, the emotions of happiness and family bliss of togetherness was the essence of love we had captured on film. Every photograph took us back in time, evoking what would otherwise be lost from a fading memory stored unreliably in our minds.

My sons asserted that it was because I had continued to speak about Ben that the memory of their father had remained alive and vivid. The younger boy reminisced often about the loving hours in his childhood spent with his father on the garden swing. The older boy remembered the time they had bonded while having their haircut together at the salon and the errands for which his father used to bring him along.

Memories are important because they bridge the past and give a sense of meaning to the present. Grief doesn't only teach us about death and loss. We learn about living, too.

When the older boy grew up, he found work in the same field as his father. He began to have a new appreciation of his father's work. Once he even had the opportunity to use his dad's published paper and applied it to his calculations in one of his work assignments. Even though his father's work had been published a long time ago, he was thrilled to learn it was still being cited today with newer studies conducted alongside it.

Two years after working for the company, he decided to pursue his Ph.D. abroad. He related to us how he was invited out to lunch with several colleagues for his farewell.

During lunch, he heard his colleagues mention someone quite senior from another company who my son happened to know. Somewhat surprised, they inquired further. He casually replied, "Oh! I knew him since I was a young child because he was one of my father's engineers."

Curious, they asked him, "What is your father's name?"

Slightly caught off guard, my son muttered clumsily, "Errr, Gan?" It sounded awkward as if he was only reiterating his own surname. He did not expect anyone would know anyway. But even then, someone immediately caught on. "Dr. Gan?"

Everyone including my son appeared astonished. Back at the office, one of his colleagues excitedly asked one of the bosses while pointing to my son, "We just found out. Do you know who his father is?"

The senior guy who was usually stern and not much of a conversationalist replied rather thoughtfully, "Yes," while looking in the direction of my son. And he continued, "I do know who his father is."

My son said he thought it felt somewhat awkward, at first. But strangely, that simple act of affirmation lifted his spirit for the rest of the week. In the book of Proverbs, King Solomon tells us: a good and honest life is a blessed memorial; but a wicked life leaves a rotten stench.[1] That feeling of immense pride in possessing a legacy of his father's good name, which bears the spirit of excellence, integrity and the remarkable person of who he was, has been utterly indescribable.

As each day passes, it reminds us that life goes on. The good news is, even though we may never forget the past, it does not mean that the past is all that we will have. Each of us can leave not just another life story, but a legacy so incredible that future generations can continue to draw from and build upon it even long after our time.

---

[1] Proverbs 10:7 (MSG)

21

It's A New Day

"What day is it?"

"It's today," squeaked Piglet.

"My favourite day," said Pooh.

I lived close to the ocean when I was growing up. Everything from the rising and lowering of tides to the hypnotic sound of waves crashing on the shore gives out an immeasurable sense of peace and blissful contentment. The sea always reminded me of the childhood friends I grew up with, those quintessential relaxing family beach vacations we used to take and carefree lazy days.

Even after we moved to the city, we returned often to the familiar "blue open spaces" we grew up around. We weaved our way out on most weekends, driving through sleepy villages and quiet stretches in search of that laid-back lifestyle found close to the soothing sound of pulsating waves and the smell of fresh, salty, ocean air. It was a short escape to the coastal towns, yet a life away, so we could disconnect from the over-stimulated state of modern-day stresses and connect with what really mattered most.

For years, I was very afraid to visit the same places that Ben and I used to enjoy, such as the beach, our favourite restaurant or even meeting the people who knew us. There was a spot off the coastal road at the beach in my hometown, which was our family's favourite. It was not until sometime in the fifth year of my grief that I found myself standing on the shoreline of the familiar ocean.

The feel of dry, sun-warmed sand under my bare feet was welcoming and delightful. I was relieved that, unlike people, it would not ask me where Ben was. I felt the acceptance of being welcomed just the same when I was with Ben as when I am now, without.

On the horizon, the tranquil pale aqua greens created a palette that was soothing and healing. The soft iridescent hues of both the ocean and the sky opened up a world of possibilities before me. In the vastness of space and ethereal beauty arises a sense of hope. Hope that I will still come to better days ahead, even when life hurts and when it makes little sense of purpose. I want to live on with hope because there is still beauty all around me that really does matter, in spite of the loss. I just needed to learn to see each day that comes to me through new eyes and a clean heart, and be receptive to the One who still holds my breath in His hands.

To be able to look up into the sky to witness the rainbow after a shower of rain or the grandeur of streaks of orange and crimson in a sunrise; the playful swirls of tangerine, pearly pinks and dusky purples that set across the firmament when evening calls and twilight falls. Though silent for a while, the dawn cracks with light once more. It gives me hope that all is well and will continue to get better down the road because there is a God who changes times and seasons. It is He who sets the stars in the skies and wraps up water in His clouds. And He will never lead us to a place where His love is not already there to sustain us. He alone is God, and He is still in control of it all.

A Hope Beyond This Life Makes Living Worthwhile

I truly believe that when you are loved, that love never ends, even when a person passes from this world onto the next. And the hope of heaven seems even sweeter because the people who have gone ahead are there. For a Christian, I believe that when someone dies, they are not gone. It is not goodbye, but I'll see you in a while.

When my mother died in the year 2000, I bought many books that were about heaven. I have no doubt she is in heaven, because like Ben, she finally made her peace with God when she decided to put her life into the hands of Christ. The hope of heaven gives me immense comfort when I think about her, of Ben and other people who have gone on ahead of me.

Not a day has passed that I have not thought about my husband. I had so many emotions hitting me at different stages in my grief. I reached the stage of *rage* at one point. Why was I so angry with that poor man who didn't choose to leave me, as if he had a choice? I don't really know. I couldn't understand my own feelings, except that I knew I was livid and had a whole lot of other emotions going on at the same time.

I remember lying on the floor of our bedroom. I kept slamming both my wrists onto the cold, tiled floor. I was sobbing so loudly that people from outside of my house could probably hear me, and I didn't care. I was done with being polite and grieving quietly. I was hurting so badly, but it wasn't from the pain that had been inflicted on my wrists; it was my heart.

I was enraged at the promise that my husband didn't keep when he told me that he would always be there to take care of me. I was mad that he was dead, and I'd been left to face the reality of living on my own now that he was gone. I was bewildered that I could feel ludicrously jealous that he got to be in heaven while I had to be in this crappy world, left to cope with everything that seemed like an overwhelming blur to me.

I also discovered that sometimes the things you know do not scare you as much as what you don't know. I began to obsess over meticulous details ahead of time. I strategized possible solutions for contingencies of things that might go wrong even way before anything could happen. I wanted to be ready and not be caught off guard or surprised from now on, I told myself. I learned soon enough that anticipating trouble or worrying ahead about what might never happen required a lot more energy, because that was like constantly throwing punches in the air all day. It was exhausting to live each day this way.

On several occasions, I contemplated suicide because even breathing hurt. I just wanted to make the pain end so badly. But each time a thought, as lucid as light, would come to me in the same moment. *What if—I killed myself, only to wake up in a different world from Ben?*

Being a Christian, I believe that as life is a gift, so is death. The Bible tells us there is a time to be born and a time to die. And time belongs to the Almighty God. The act of suicide can only end the present circumstances to the worldly troubles, but it doesn't determine where our soul will continue to live on in the afterlife. It is a very sobering thought that human beings have a beginning and no ending; that every person who is born can never cease to exist because the soul cannot die.

In the last-quarter century, many accounts of people's experiences during clinical death have been documented. Both ancient religious stories, as well as doctors' contemporary research, reiterate that after the death of the body, the soul [the personality or consciousness, or *the me*] continues to hear, think and feel in a new surrounding. The accounts of near-death experiences, including the clinically dead, reported either to have arrived at a loathsome place filled with terror or a realm that was blissful, bright and joyful.

I truly believe that this world significantly prepares us for the next. We may not understand all the things that happen to us now, but someday everything will be clear. Death becomes a relief, and is not to be feared when it's Jesus who meets us at the end of the road. It's graduation! It's a homecoming! It's a *reward.*

And so, for difficult days when everything feels like work, and there's little sense in meaning or purpose, the hope of heaven keeps me on. It helps me to turn to God and to rest in His promises. As C.S. Lewis said, all the beauty and joy of planet earth represent "only the scent of a flower we have not found, the echo of a tune we have not heard, news from a country we have never visited."

Life will go on, even if it'll never be quite the same.

Having a perspective of heaven does not mean I value any less the human life I now possess. It does not take away the purpose of living because life is for the living. To see the value of life as a gift and not a burden enables me to live *more* fully rather than less. It teaches me how to live as deeply as I have learned how to love.

Death is hard for the people left behind. When a spouse or a child dies, we never stop loving them. If love never ends, why would we expect our grief to end?

Steven King wrote in *Bag of Bones*, "This is how we go on: one day at a time, one meal at a time, one pain at a time, one breath at a time." But there is hope that someday again, the sun will shine. The day will seem brighter. Life will go on, even if it'll never be quite the same.

Make Each Day Count

In his book *Coaching at End of Life*, Don Eisenhauer wrote, "Walking the journey of grief is life-changing. No one chooses to experience grief. It is almost always unwanted and unplanned. Yet, for many, the journey of grief is a wonderfully growing experience."

At no time in our life schedule is there ever a suitable time for it. I would do anything to have Ben back here with me. Nothing

Edwin's fun time at the beach

Watching over my children, as always

I have learned is worth him being gone. Yet I have learned a lot. I have grown in measures far beyond what I could ever have imagined.

Through my grief, I learned life is a gift that is too precious to waste another minute of it being pessimistic, judgmental and fault-finding. I forgive myself for all the mistakes I have made when I didn't know better. And I forgive all others for theirs, whether they want it or not.

I have learned to accept my own uniqueness and live out the most authentic version that I am. I learn to make each day count. I learn to smile and laugh again. I learn to wake up giving praise for another day and for the gift of life that I did nothing to earn. I learn to take care of myself. I choose to see the abundance in what life has for me and not dwell on the lack of it. I have learned that though I am alone, I don't have to be lonely. I still have things to do, places to go, languages to learn and hobbies to indulge in. I discovered that it's not the absence of people that makes me lonely, but only keeping company with the wrong ones.

Even though I can stay quite contentedly a social recluse, I have learned the importance of community. When I had the opportunity to serve as a guitarist in my local church, I thought I had finally found my niche because it was something that I enjoyed doing. Over time, as I developed the little that I have, it became more. I began to see more areas of my life being developed when I became willing to step out to do more than what is comfortable for me. The more I gave of myself to others, the more I gained in ways I have never expected.

It may be music or writing for me, but it may be working with children or volunteering to work in the community food kitchen for someone else. Only you can determine what it is, but you will not know until you give yourself a chance to find that out. Give it a go when you get a kick in your gut, or when an opportunity in the area of your innate gift is being called out or required. The thing is to stay open. You will be pleasantly surprised, as more areas may very well develop when you stay committed to doing good in giving and serving others with fervency over time.

I found joy in serving, as it has not only taught me discipline, humility and the importance of staying committed to a specific cause; most importantly, it has kept me connected to other people. It has taught me that though we grieve alone, we heal in a community. We learn to work with people, we learn to care for others, and we give back.

I learn to value each day more than ever before. I learn to cultivate the ability to notice and appreciate the ordinary and small little things I have so often missed in the past, when they often come disguised as chores, routines and even mindless tasks. And sometimes, it takes the little child in us to teach every weary adult that there is laughter hiding in every moment, joy in every second and love in every single breath.

Afterword: Reflections

"Blue, too, is a true colour of the season."

—Rev Nancy Taylor

It is the eleven-year anniversary of my husband's death this week as I work on the one-year revision to this book. I am keenly aware that it's the holiday season once again. For some, it's the most exciting time of the year, but for those whose loved ones are no longer here, December can be the hardest. As both my sons and my own birthday happen to fall in the last quarter of the year, the swell of grief starts surfacing even months before December. To think that, after knowing so much more on the subject of grieving and mourning for a loved one, as well as on depression and ways to cope, than I did before, it can still knock me off kilter.

December is the month I dread most as merriment fills the air with joyful Christmas music and displays of dazzling, colourful, festive lights and ornaments. As the season approaches, the emotions of nostalgia, of being deprived, yearnings, vulnerability, strength, apprehension and possibly more remain perplexing and heightened.

Christmas is a time that warms your heart like a mug of hot cocoa. It wraps itself around you like a shawl with a reflective mood of another year gone by. It's that time of the year, which is deemed special for many people, that can cause more aches and frayed nerves than any other time of the year. Could it be that we sometimes try too hard to achieve happiness and a sense of 'all is well' simply for the sake of others? The result is, if we do things in the wrong sort of way, it makes us miserable, angry and confused. It leaves us with a greater sense of guilt and failure, rather than good.

It was the day before Christmas. I was just about to pull the shades down to sleep the rest of the afternoon away when I received a text from Don, a family friend who asked how my day was going. He reckoned it was understandably difficult as it was the holidays. He was only too familiar with the grief emotions himself, after experiencing the loss of his father.

I told him how I had decided to do something different this year. Instead of avoiding the holidays, or participating in them half-heartedly as I had done since my spouse died, I decided to *embrace* Christmas and the New Year celebrations. I have grown and learned so much in this journey of grief and widowhood that I truly believed I was ready to get back into the mainstream of people and activities. So I dressed up and went to church.

I love my church and the people. They are the most wonderful folks that spell 'family' for me. My time at church started out great, but midway, I became more and more overwhelmed. There was a sense of excitement in the air to welcome both the old and new friends who have made it home from all over to celebrate the holidays. Though I had gone that morning with the intention to mingle and share the holiday spirit with friends at church, I had not expected to be overwhelmed instead by that deep sense of missing and the absence of my own family that morning. It made me realise I was not as ready to celebrate this holiday as I thought I was. I was once again reminded how foolish it is to have any assumptions about grief at all.

"How long does it take for grief to truly end?" I messaged Don back.

"Grief *never* ends," he replied in text. "You just allow yourself to feel all that you do now. Your grief is a result of your deep love and close relationship with Ben."

I realise now, the yuletide is a special hell for those families whose ache resurfaces, triggered by the empty chairs, missing faces and the silent voices that haunt the holidays. For those whose loved ones have died, it is simply a painful reminder of an ache arising from a love that never ages.

Ben died in the first week of January, so December is always going to be difficult. That sense of deep aching was felt during our son's graduation and also at our son's wedding some years back. In both events, I held my breath and simply kept going, trying so hard not to fall apart. But December, *this* is an old, recurring foe. I learned now that I don't have to fight it. I just needed to do things *differently*. I needed to do what is going to help me.

It made me realise that even eleven years after my spouse's death, the vulnerability to experience grief is always with me. Even though my feelings of loss continue to change shape over time, it does not mean that time can fix the void of my loved one's absence.

Speaking to my friend Don that afternoon helped me understand that grief is an ongoing process. It never ends because you never stop loving them. As love never dies, neither does grief, as the effects of that one finite loss show in ripples throughout different phases over a lifetime. We just continue to grow in the midst of it. But because I know deep sorrow, I also know that there is nothing I will ever take for granted. What I have experienced with Ben, my best friend, husband and father to my children—even death cannot take away.

Felicia G. Y. Lam

2 January 2019

References

Bennett, Roy T. *The Light in the Heart: Inspirational Thoughts for Living Your Best Life.* Roy Bennett. 2016. Kindle.

Lewis, C.S. *A Grief Observed.* London: Faber and Faber. 1961.

Lewis, C.S. *The Weight of Glory and Other Addresses.* New York: The Macmillan Company. 1949.

Eisenhauer, Don. *Coaching at End of Life: A Coach Approach to Ministering to the Dying and the Grieving.* Coaching4Clergy. 2012.

Eisenhauer, Don. *Life Lessons from dragonflies: Helping us face the inevitable end of life issues.* PDF edition. 2012.

Daly, Tim, Colm Feore, Debrah Farentino, Casey Siemaszko, Jeffrey De Munn, Craig R. Baxley, Thomas H. Brodek, and Stephen King. *Stephen King's Storm of the Century.* United States: Trimark Home Video. 1999.

Gilbert, Elizabeth. *Eat, Pray, Love: One Woman's Search for Everything Across Italy, India and Indonesia.* New York: Penguin. 2010.

Gladwell, Malcom. *David and Goliath: Underdogs, Misfits, and the Art of Battling Giants.* Boston: Little, Brown and Company. 2013.

King, Stephen. *Bag of Bones.* New York: Scribner. 1998.

Kubler-Ross, Elisabeth. *On Death and Dying,* London: Routledge, 1973.

Lutzer, Erwin W. *One Minute After You Die.* Moody Publishers, Chicago, 1997.

Schimelpfening, Nancy. *Beyond Sadness: Is It Clinical Depression or Sadness?* 2003.

Trivedi J.K., Himanshu Sareen, and Mohan Dhyani. "Psychological Aspects of Widowhood and Divorce." In *Some Issues in Women's Studies, and Other Essays* (A.R. Singh and S.A. Singh, eds.), MSM, 7, Jan - Dec 2009, pp 37-49.

Moody, Raymond. *Life after Life*, Mockingbird Books, 1975.

Sandberg, Sheryl, and Adam M. Grant. *Option B: facing adversity, building resilience, and finding joy.* New York: Alfred A. Knopf. 2017. PDF version.

Gallery

Ben's love for motorcycles

Ben (rider) with friend (pillion passenger) performing motorcycle stunts

Me, a toddler, in the backyard of my childhood home

Traditional tea ceremony, a sign of gratitude and respect to the elder(s) of the family

Happiness is in the little things: Coffee with my eldest son, Sydney 2018

My boys are all grown up now: North Wollongong Beach, 2018

The view outside my window reminding me there is beauty even in the midst of pain

Made in the
USA
Lexington, KY

55646529R00083